LINCOLN**

Teashop Walks

Roger Fox

COUNTRYSIDE BOOKS
NEWBURY, BERKSHIRE

C000277243

First published 2000
© Roger Fox 2000

All rights reserved. No reproduction
permitted without the prior permission
of the publisher:

COUNTRYSIDE BOOKS
3 Catherine Road
Newbury, Berkshire

To view our complete range of books,
please visit us at
www.countrysidebooks.co.uk

ISBN 1 85306 627 3

Designed by Graham Whiteman
Maps and photographs by the author

Produced through MRM Associates Ltd., Reading
Printed by Woolnough Bookbinding Ltd., Irthlingborough

Contents

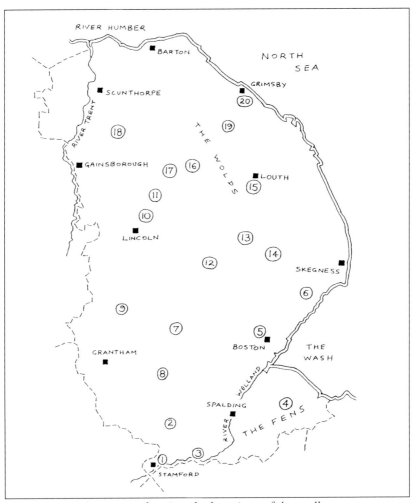

Area map showing the locations of the walks.

KEY TO SKETCH MAPS

The walk	— — — →	Railway	+++++	Churches		
Other path or track	• • • • •	River or stream	ꭓꭓꭓ	Building referred to		
Road	═══	Pond, lake or sea		Teashop		
Car park	P			Point in text	③	

Walk

Introduction

'Kirkby with Muckby-cum-Sparrowby-cum-Spinx
Is down a long lane in the county of Lincs,
And often on Wednesdays, well-harnessed and spruce,
I would drive into Wiss over Winderby Sluice.
A whacking great sunset bathed level and drain
From Kirkby with Muckby to Beckby-on-Bain.'

None of the villages in Sir John Betjeman's *A Lincolnshire Tale* exist of course, but the county must have made enough of an impression on him to sit down and write this atmospheric verse. Such imaginative place names conjure up an image of Lincolnshire as a rather ancient and timeless county. In fact it is blissfully so and much more. It is a land of infinite variety and something of everything.

Given that Lincolnshire is England's second largest county it remains a remarkably well kept secret. The town of Stamford, at the southernmost tip, is actually nearer to London than to the River Humber, which forms the county's northern border. The Rivers Trent and Welland roughly trace the western and southern limits, while the waves of the North Sea break upon its eastern shores. Historically divided into the three 'ridings' of Kesteven, Lindsey and Holland, Lincolnshire is naturally split into three lowland bands by the chalk hills of the Wolds in the east (the highest hills in the Eastern Counties) and the limestone Lincoln Cliff in the west. The low coastal plain merges into the broad levels of the Fens, which occupy the entire south-eastern quadrant of the county.

These geographical separations lead to a diversity of scenery which makes for ideal walking territory. The wide horizons are punctuated by such landmarks as the Humber Bridge and Grimsby's Dock Tower in the north and Boston Stump in the south. But the most breathtaking break in the skyline is Lincoln Cathedral itself, the unmistakable outline of its triple towers visible for many miles around. The county is particularly well endowed in masterpieces of church architecture, and even the smallest village boasts a noteworthy example. I must confess to a passion for the churches of the area, which will become evident as you read the following pages – I hope you will forgive this obsession and perhaps come to share it.

The county is rich in other historical relics too, from the Roman Ermine Street to the numerous aviation heritage sites that tell of Lincolnshire's huge importance in the Second World War. A cobweb of abandoned railway lines covers the county, and as well as track beds and tunnels, the countryside is littered with old carriages which have found new employment as farm shelters and stores, evidence that the axe of Dr Beeching was wielded more ferociously over Lincolnshire than most areas. Pretty water mills can be found throughout the county, and dark tar-covered windmill towers contrast with the white sails and balconies, with mills of four, five, six and eight sails located around the area.

It is in some of these buildings that many of Lincolnshire's best little teashops thrive, often as part of a larger set-up. Others, of course, prosper in their own right, relying solely upon the reputation they have built. These chapters encompass the whole teashop spectrum, from the humble and voluntary to the most splendid. They each have their own character, even if some do not conform to the traditional idea of a teashop. The thing they do all have in common is that they serve an extremely good cup of tea. Beyond that, their merits for inclusion vary from their setting and the treasures of the walks based around them to the character and enthusiasm of their owners. All are happy to cater for large groups, providing that they are warned in advance of your arrival. But please check with the teashop owners before you park on their premises then head into the countryside – many have only limited parking space.

However, there is no such thing as a 'free lunch', and you now have to earn yours. You will find that the walks reflect the variety of the landscape, ranging from simple village strolls to full day expeditions through the countryside. Some are circular, some 'there-and-back' and some figure-of-eight, but all end up back at the starting point. Most start and end at the teashop, but different ideas for starting points are included. Each walk can be tailored to suit your inclinations, with short-cuts evident on the maps, and some suggested extensions included. In all cases the use of the corresponding Ordnance Survey map is strongly recommended. As well as clarifying your route in far more detail than the maps in the book can, they contain a wealth of additional information to make the walks much more rewarding. Map numbers are given, along with the grid references. A prior visit to a nearby Tourist Information Centre will also benefit you and add to your enjoyment of the walk.

Although some of the walks are hilly and some lengthy there is nothing to daunt the walker of average competence. My son, who is six years old, has helped me to complete all the walks, and I hope that there is plenty to interest all children. The routes avoid busy roads where possible, but awareness of safety is important, especially when there are young children doing the walk.

You should not expect to find the neatly trimmed and labelled paths you might find in a National Park. Here the paths are free and open, not tampered with and truly rural. You might have to share your path with tractors and farmers – this is an agricultural area and a working landscape. You can often walk for miles and not see another soul, and can usually have the whole scene to yourself. This is the beauty of an area not normally associated with walking, and it is with some reluctance that the secret of these undiscovered byways is shared. There is nothing more peaceful than a countryside walk in the crisp early morning air or under the ever-reddening hues of a vast Lincolnshire sunset. Different seasons, too, lead to different pleasures. Fields of dazzling yellow oilseed, patches of scarlet poppies and seas of blue flax alternate spectacularly, while daffodils, bluebells, snowdrops and golden corn add to this colourful picture. Field paths that may be difficult to follow in summer when the corn is high become clearly revealed again after harvest time. And in winter – as well as the chance of a glorious snow-covered setting – buildings and views that are hidden from sight by the fullness of summer greenery are visible through the bare trees. See how many times you say 'I didn't see that last time'.

So if you love cakes and countryside, pull on your walking boots and treat yourself to a brisk walk along the green lanes of Lincolnshire, followed by a reviving tea at one of these welcoming halts. Or reverse the order and burn off those calories after your lunch. Either way I hope that this book will be a friendly companion to you – even if you are walking alone. And of all the 'friendly companions' in this noble county who have helped me to write it, I should mention a special debt of gratitude to Julie, who suffered in silence, and Harry, who just suffered!

Roger Fox

Walk 1
STAMFORD

Here is a walk that offers the best of both worlds – and three counties! Stamford needs no introduction, but we'll give it one anyway. This is England's best preserved stone town, still based upon a medieval street pattern of winding roads, cobbled squares and narrow passageways. It is a masterpiece of Georgian architecture and ancient churches built of local limestone, and has been an inspiration to writers and artists alike. Best of all the River Welland penetrates into the heart of the town, and it is through the water meadows along her banks that you make your escape into the tranquillity of the countryside. Over hilly terrain then to explore two lovely villages (in neighbouring Rutland and Northamptonshire), before you allow the Welland to lazily guide you back into the lively town.

☕ Stamford is full of small squares surrounded by exquisite stone buildings. Red Lion Square is busier than most – positively bustling on market days – and The Central Restaurant, Bakery and Tearooms, reputed to be part of a 15th century great wool house, dominates the finest corner of the square. Curved windows, full of 'goodies', entice you into the timber-framed building, and you pass through the bakery to a crooked staircase. The narrowing steps lead you past stained-glass windows set in carved stone to the tearooms proper. Traditional and surprisingly large, the sense of grandeur is enhanced by a beamed ceiling, carved oak panelling and stone walls. It is easy to believe that the same family of wealthy wool merchants, the Brownes, who founded the nearby All Saints' church and the hospital in Broad Street, also created this building, used as a restaurant since the 1900s. Please ensure that you are accompanied by a healthy appetite when you enter. Everything you would expect from a large teashop is on offer and much more besides. A suggestion might be to select something substantial from the range of lunches (leek and Roquefort cannelloni, possibly) then simply take one of everything from the downstairs bakery home with you! Oddly, the house speciality is the 'Yorkshire' curd tart. The Central is open from 9.30 am to 5 pm on Sunday to Thursday and 8 am to 5 pm on Friday and Saturday, all year round. Telephone: 01780 763217. However, should you manage to find the tearooms closed Stamford is full of restaurants and inns serving good food.

DISTANCE: 5½ miles.

MAPS: OS Landranger 141 (Kettering and Corby) or Explorer 15 (234) (Rutland Water).

STARTING POINT: The walk begins at the tearooms in Red Lion Square (GR 029071). Parking, however, is limited in Stamford town centre and you should park on the other side of the River Welland in the Station Road car park (GR 029068).

HOW TO GET THERE: Stamford is easily reached from north or south, being just a mile from the A1. To reach the Station Road car park, approach from the south and turn left at the traffic lights by the George Hotel. From the car park cross the Meadows and climb into Red Lion Square via Sheepmarket.

ALTERNATIVES: The villages of Easton-on-the-Hill (point 4) and Tinwell (point 6) offer you easier parking than Stamford town centre, and would both be excellent bases for the walk to include the teashop as a halfway refreshment stop.

THE WALK

1. A short passageway to the side of the Bakery leads you into Sheepmarket and along Castle Dyke into Bath Row. Now cross the footbridge in front of you over the millstream into the Meadows (as though heading back to the car park). You should not spend too long feeding the ducks and watching young fishermen waiting for roach and eels to bite, but turn right across these lawns and head for a gate next to the River Welland. Over a more untamed meadow and through another gate, you will see the Boudicca Monument on your left.

The vital Roman link from London to Lincoln and York crossed the River Welland at a ford here, the only point guaranteeing a year-round crossing. In AD 61 survivors of the ninth Roman legion, pursued by Queen Boudicca, fled this way. Following the ford's demise a lower crossing was preferred, now the stone bridge around which Stamford has grown.

Continue along this path by the winding Welland for some distance until a gated metal footbridge (Broadeng Bridge) takes you to the river's opposite bank.

2. A few yards further along this bank another path branches left, away from the river, and through the thistles towards a clear tunnel under the A1. You emerge from this tunnel into daylight and an idyllic rural scene. Over a short field, ascend a planked walkway to the busy railway line linking Stamford with Leicester.

3. Taking great care to check that it is safe, cross and descend the other bank via more 'plankways'. When the undergrowth recedes, you find yourself at the edge of a large field. Your path, however, is clear and climbs a steepening hill to a wide track between two enchanting woods. When this track turns sharp left you continue straight ahead, but pause to glance at the jagged skyline behind you, a glorious panorama of the spires and towers of Stamford. The footpath through the next field jumps over a stile, then another, to bring you onto the private lawn of a large house on your left. You exit by the far left-hand corner onto Church Street next to the stunning – but until now unseen – church of All Saints in Easton-on-the-Hill.

The picturesque village of Easton-on-the-Hill, in Northamptonshire, does warrant an exploration. Of its many fine stone buildings the church is the finest. Overlooking the valley from its hilltop site, the tower is crowned by four remarkable decorated pinnacles, each one rising to a dazzling golden weathervane. The interior, well lit by large clear windows, contains a 'dumb organist', the ecclesiastical equivalent of a barrel-organ, an ingenious but short-lived solution to the shortage of organists in 1849.

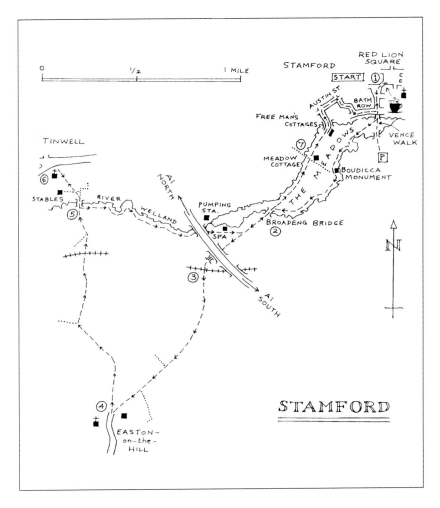

4. Having thoroughly inspected Easton and its church you now head north along Church Street, through a kissing-gate and down the hill. Note that the fields here are all lined by tumbledown drystone walls – a most unusual feature in the Lincolnshire landscape. Excellent views again unfold, both towards Stamford and the famous quarry at nearby Ketton. The lane becomes a field path again and, where the boundary hedge veers left, you head half-right down the hill and through the field towards the right-hand corner of the wood ahead. Curiously, this arable field is peppered with fine solitary trees, which make a wonderful spectacle against the patterned fields beyond. A view to admire – a nightmare to plough! The edge of the wood leads you back to the railway. Once more, cross with the utmost care and enter the next field. In the far corner the path grows into a track and curves to meet the River Welland at a concrete bridge.

5. Ahead of you is the village of Tinwell. Over the bridge, cross a stile immediately on your left and walk diagonally over the grass (crossing the gravel track) to identify a hidden stile in the opposite corner between a fence and conifer trees. Beyond this, clearly visible is the lovely ancient church in the centre of Tinwell, well worth an extension to the walk. There are several other interesting stone buildings in the village, including a smithy with a huge arch in the shape of a horseshoe.

6. Leaving Tinwell, return as far as the other side of the river and simply meander back with it, admiring the groups of trees on the far bank, until you once again pass under the A1. Ironically, these dark, arched tunnels are the only place where the busy A1 seems silent. Continue past the modern weir and pumping-station (which supplies Rutland Water) and examine the old spa which appears on your left.

The 'pepperpot' head you see was placed here in 1864, by order of John Paradise. The mineral spring had been brought into use in 1819, when the ironwater was sought after by sufferers of a whole range of ailments, in the belief that it had medicinal properties. The well head was renovated in 1994.

Past the spa you rejoin your outgoing path, and backtrack as far as the iron footbridge, which you cross. This time, leave the riverbank and head straight across the Meadows in the direction of a gate by the red-ivy-clad Meadow Cottage.

7. The walk here upgrades to an attractive paved and railed stream-side path named 'Melancholy Walk'. At 'Free Man's Cottages' the route crosses the millstream into Austin Friars Lane, then right into Austin Street and right again into King's Mill Lane. This lovely winding lane, narrow and cobbled, leads you down past superb stone buildings and arches and back into Bath Row. From here you can see that the car park is only a short walk away, across the bridges and Meadows one last time, with the temptations of the Central also now within easy reach.

Walk 2
BOURNE

Bourne is an attractive market town built around a natural well between the black-soiled Fens and wooded countryside. As the birthplace of Hereward the Wake, its history is naturally colourful, embracing successive occupations by Romans and Normans, the rise and fall of an Augustinian abbey and a disastrous 16th century uprising. Your walk accesses open land via a 'secret passage' and reaches its climax with the exciting sculpture trail in the ancient Bourne Wood.

Strolling along North Street it is easy to miss the unassuming façade of Polly's, a 'Typical English Teashop of High Repute'. It is not a particularly old or exceptional building, but once inside you will find a popular and busy teashop where locals and visitors mingle. Black and white photographs of Bourne adorn the long wall but pride of place is held by the display of tempting desserts – all home-made. From the extensive range of lunches you might select the 'Pig-in-a-blanket'

(sausage and omelette), and with your afternoon tea, a 'Wet Nelly' is a highly recommended Eccles cake. Polly's is open on Monday to Saturday from 8 am till 4.30 pm and on Sundays from 10 am to 4 pm. And who is 'Polly'? Polly put the kettle on, of course. Telephone: 01778 425627. The Nag's Head and the Angel in the Market Place also serve food.

DISTANCE: 5 miles.
MAPS: OS Landranger 130 (Grantham) or Explorer 248 (Bourne and Heckington).
STARTING POINT: Polly's tearoom in Bourne (GR 096203).
HOW TO GET THERE: Bourne is on the A15 midway between Sleaford and Peterborough. Polly's is central, on your left as you leave the town centre travelling north. Parking nearby is possible but limited, and you should follow signs for public car parking in the town.
ALTERNATIVES: Park in Bourne Wood (point 5) and take tea in the middle of the walk. It is worth time to explore the woodland and the sculpture trail fully.

THE WALK

1. From the teashop walk through the Market Place into South Street, passing on your left the ingeniously designed Town Hall, and turn left when you reach Church Lane. After a few yards this lane bends right and on your left you are now confronted by the vast wall of stone belonging to the Abbey Church of St Peter and St Paul, with a tiny stream opposite.

The church contains all that remains of an Augustinian abbey, founded in 1138. The abbey served until 1536, when dissolution befell it with only ten canons in residence. An uprising led by Sir John Thimbleby, a prominent local Catholic and landowner, failed to save the abbey, and of the living quarters nothing remains. However, much of the early architecture, including four huge round Norman piers, can still be seen.

Past the church an alleyway leads you back into South Street. Turn right, cross, and walk as far as Baldock's Mill on your left. Inside, fascinating exhibitions and models have replaced the old corn milling machinery. A passageway through the mill opens onto a picturesque spot alongside the Bourne Eau, and you follow the delightful riverside path until it broadens to a grassy lawn near to the old well head.

The well head of Saint Peter's Pool is a natural feature consisting of a circular clay-lined pool filled by seven springs. The Romans based a fortress next to this well and the castle was developed in medieval times by Baldwin Fitz Gilbert, Lord of the Manor and the founder of the abbey.

15

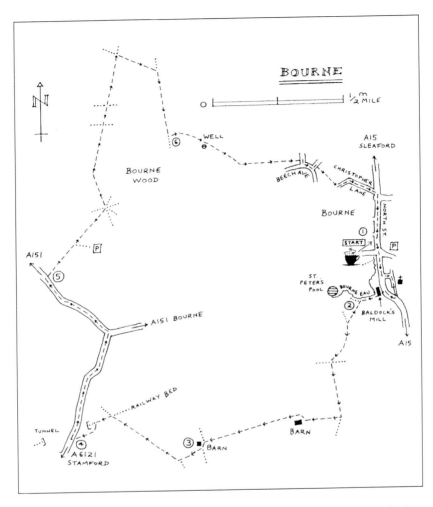

2. Now look carefully for a solitary tree on your left, behind which a hidden path drops through the undergrowth and to a stile. Head half-right over the field to find another stile, then follow the next field edge left, with woods deepening to the side. Past the bed of a former railway, the path now continues inside the edge of these woods until it meets a gravel track. Turn right and follow this track past one large barn to a smaller one with a black barrel roof.

3. Behind this barn a wide swathe of grass leads across a field, then steers right, crosses a small ditch and continues to the course of an old railway. Over a wooden fence to your left, dive immediately right into the trees and look carefully for a set of wooden steps descending the embankment to the track-bed. To your left now is the yawning mouth of a formidable tunnel, but before you reach it you are relieved to find another flight of wooden steps leading you back up the left-hand bank. At the top continue right along the inside edge of the wood to a main road.

4. Turn right to follow this road to a major junction, then left until the road reaches the entrance to Bourne Wood on the right.

Bourne Wood is a remnant of the primeval Forest of Brunswald, and oak, ash, beech and elm have covered this site for 2,000 years. The wood is criss-crossed by a maze of forest tracks, along which bluebells, primroses and wood anemones are found in spring. If silent and alert you may also spot fallow deer, foxes, squirrels and woodpeckers. Easier to locate is the fascinating series of unusual sculptures, begun in 1991, some of which you will chance upon during your foray.

5. The entrance road into the wood leads straight to a major meeting of paths at the wooden sculpture of 'The Woodsman'. Select carefully – it is the wide gravel track to your left that you want. If you do not soon pass 'The Window in the Wood' on your left, you should reconsider your choice! In ½ mile, look for a milestone depicting a number of mediaeval horrors to your right. Here a grassy path leads you down to the 'Shelter Skelter'. Turn right again, pass 'The Crows', and continue until you see a sign indicating a footpath on the left. This in turn leads over a stile and out of the woods.

6. Midway across the next pasture is a blind well, supposedly flowing with beneficial mineral water and surrounded, curiously, by a series of submerged kitchen sinks – I counted twenty! Leave this field by another stile and follow a long fenced passage to Hazelwood Drive – turn right then left into Beech Avenue. Shortly enter Orchard Close on your left and look for an immediate footpath on the right. This path improves as you progress, eventually emerging as Christopher Lane near the town centre once more. The whistling kettle of Polly's is now just a few minutes walk to your right.

Walk 3
MARKET DEEPING

This is a walk from a small town on the edge of the Fens with many fine stone buildings, especially in the imposing Market Place. Market Deeping's prosperity and importance as a staging post on the road from London to Lincoln is evident from a number of old coaching inns. Clinging to the River Welland as it winds along the Northamptonshire border, the walk takes you from a stone-built town to a stone-built village and back via a choice of return routes. A mainly rural circuit, the riverside paths are level, if often muddy, but the reward of a delicious tea in the French-style tearoom is well worth the effort.

 Inside one of the many fine stone buildings which line Church Street you will come across a tiny slice of the Mediterranean. La Maison Gourmande Patisserie and Bakery has a distinctly French flavour, and everything is baked on the premises. Just try saying 'non' to the display of creamy cakes and gateaux, with a mountain of meringues and bread loaves behind. Hot croissants, quiches and pancakes, all with savoury fillings, are much in demand, as are a range of exotic salads. Less French, but equally tasty, is Sunday lunch – but you must book. You can choose to sit in one of two rooms, or in good weather relax outside on the small patio area, next to the fishpond. La Maison Gourmande is open from 7.30 am to 4 pm, Wednesdays to Sundays, but is closed during January and February. Telephone: 01778 344719. When the Patisserie is not open Market Deeping is well stocked with inns and places to eat.

DISTANCE: 5½ miles.

MAPS: OS Landranger 142 (Peterborough) or Explorer 235 (Wisbech and Peterborough North).

STARTING POINT: La Maison Gourmande in Market Deeping (GR 138102).

HOW TO GET THERE: Market Deeping is situated on the southern limits of the county where the A15 and the A16 meet. From the Market Place La Maison Gourmande is a few yards along Church Street on the left. You can usually park on the road outside, but there are public car parks behind the shops if not.

ALTERNATIVES: West Deeping (point 3) would also make an ideal base for the walk. The teashop is then reached halfway round. From either starting point there is a choice of routes at point 5, where you can opt to follow the main A16 into Market Deeping.

THE WALK

1. From the teashop head into Deeping's grand Market Place with its impressive stone-fronted buildings, and cross the graceful three-arched bridge over the River Welland.

It is the River Welland which unites The Deepings, a cluster of five stone villages which line its banks as it flows towards The Wash on the east coast. Once a trade link, small boats and barges would ply back and forth along the river. Looking at the winding Welland today it is hard to imagine that it was navigable until 1860.

Over a stile on the right walk back to the bank and turn left to follow the clear waters of the river – you are to be close companions for the next 2½ miles. Beyond a new bypass, sections of the riverbank may be undergoing renovation work and you should walk behind the trees nearby. Now into open countryside, the ducks have given way to wild swans, herons and wood pigeons. Rabbits and foxes may also be seen. And conkers! Horse chestnut trees occur throughout the walk and each autumn make this conker country indeed, delighting children and

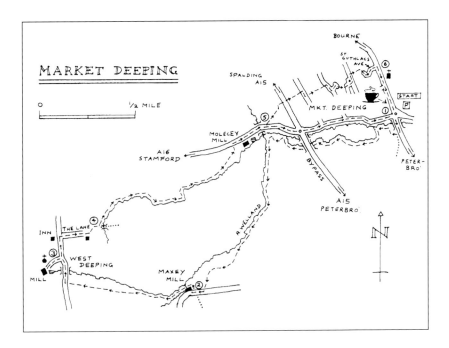

offering dads a brief chance of a second childhood. The winding Welland eventually leads you to a gate. Heed the electric fence here and veer instead to your left to follow a lesser stream, often dry, alongside a hedgerow. Soon a wooden bridge brings you onto a road and, turning right, you quickly arrive at Maxey Mill. This splendid old stone corn mill, built in 1779, still displays many original features.

2. Crossing a stile to the right of the mill a footpath takes you to the mill pond behind, and an even more charming scene. The path hurdles a small sluice-bridge before continuing on a wooded bank between two watercourses to a stile. Not even the smell from the nearby piggery could taint this wonderful setting! Continue along a field path with the river to your right and tall trees swaying on the opposite bank. At the end of a long, narrow pasture a white wooden gate brings you onto a road. Now turn right and cross a narrow stone bridge into West Deeping. The views here are stunning and you will want to explore Church Lane as far as the beautiful watermill and St Andrew's church.

3. Back on the road you will be surprised by the wealth of handsome stone buildings as you continue through the village. Opposite the 200-

year-old Red Lion Inn, 'The Lane' leads you to a farm next to Cromwell House. Cross the courtyard of neat green buildings and exit via the opposite corner.

4. Descend to a stream, but before the bridge divert left and follow a good farm track left, keeping the stream on your right. In ½ mile the track dwindles to a single narrow path, and in another ½ mile leaves the stream to negotiate a route along a wire fence with some difficulty. The path widens for the last hundred yards, reaching the road at a stile. Now follow this road right and pass the imposing Georgian façade of Molecey House and the adjacent mill set in well-maintained grounds.

5. Over the next bridge you must choose. The easy option takes you directly into the heart of Market Deeping along this road (the A16). A more adventurous and rewarding trail takes you over the gate to your left (which appears to have remained unopened for decades) and diagonally across two fields to reach the bypass on a path alongside a low hedge. The path continues on the other side of this busy road, crossing a field and turning right when it meets the next road. Then turn left along a muddy passage and, reaching Tattershall Drive, turn right. The next cul-de-sac on your left leads to a short passage into Green Walk. Turning left, skirt round a small grass island and look for a paved walk guarded by bollards on the other side of the road in front of you. Passing a row of new cottages on the left, this path brings you to St Guthlac Avenue, which in turn leads you onto Church Street, near to St Guthlac's church itself.

St Guthlac was an Anglo-Saxon hermit who came to nearby Crowland in AD 669, and the church dedicated to him in Deeping dates as far back as the 12th century. The square tower has a pair of unusual sundials on its north and south faces – one declaring 'The day is thine' and the other 'The night cometh'. Behind is the huge 14th century Rectory, believed to be the oldest inhabited parsonage in England.

6. Continuing past the church (the town centre is now less than ½ mile away) and while you wait for the delicacies you have ordered at the Maison Gourmande to arrive, time to count up who collected the most conkers!

Walk 4
FLEET HARGATE

For some people the Fens are an acquired taste. But look to these far horizons and vast endless skies, and you will find a wealth of wonderful views. This is a land of moods and atmospheres, particularly striking at sundown or dawn. Across the fields dotted settlements stand out against islands of trees, ever hazier as they recede into the distance, and the spires and towers of churches in every village for miles around can be seen. Your walk leads you into the heart of fenland, where a quiet rural footpath links two outstanding village churches, both dedicated to the same saint, but each unique. And between these two elongated parishes of Fleet and Gedney is a lovely teashop in a sleepy village now bypassed by modern life.

Along the old main road in Fleet Hargate – nowadays quiet – trees sway behind a high brick wall leading down to The Willow Tearooms. Hanging flower baskets compete for attention with the frontage decked in blue and white. Inside you will find a traditional warm welcome and a marvellous display of cream gateaux and puddings that, if you are there at lunchtime, may make you want to skip your main course. You should not. A range of delicious hot and cold meals is available (try the chilli toasties!) and Sunday lunch is so popular as to make booking essential. Only then should you choose between the truffle cake and that tiramisu. It's all home-made and served in clean, attractive surroundings. Little passing trade means that here reputation counts. The Willow Tearooms are open all year round from 10.30 am to 5 pm on Wednesday to Saturday and noon to 5 pm on Sundays. Telephone: 01406 423112. When the tearooms are closed there are two inns in the village serving food, and Holbeach is only 2 miles away.

DISTANCE: 3 miles.

MAPS: OS Landranger 131 (Boston and Spalding) or Explorer 249 (Spalding and Holbeach).

STARTING POINT: The Willow Tearooms in Fleet Hargate (GR 398249).

HOW TO GET THERE: Travel east along the A17 towards King's Lynn and 2 miles past the turn for Holbeach turn right onto the B1515. Turn immediately left into Fleet Hargate and in less than ½ mile find The Willow Tearooms on your left. There is some parking available, but you should park on the road nearby.

ALTERNATIVES: Enjoy the teashop during the walk by parking at the church in Fleet. To extend the walk you could continue south across the fields beyond Fleet or proceed on the footpath past the church at Gedney, over the main A17 then across the countryside to Gedney Dyke.

THE WALK

1. From the teashop head west along the main road through Fleet Hargate, passing interesting buildings on either side, the best being the grand Fleet House. After ½ mile, at a shop on your right, turn left into Hocklesgate.

2. Having passed through a housing area Hocklesgate quickly changes into a quiet country road, with wide views over the open fields. Rather than grain, the fields around you are full of all types of vegetables, flowers and fruit. Rows of greenhouses and cloches lead the eye to the horizon, where the church at Fleet is now prominent. Ignoring a left fork at a double-bend, continue to York House, where you can identify the former railway line to Spalding – look to left and right to spot old railway buildings on the roads parallel to Hocklesgate. Continue into Fleet itself and, where the road bends left into Wood Street at a cheerfully decorated school, the unusual thatched lychgate of the church comes into view.

The stone church of Mary Magdalen in Fleet is remarkable for its detached tower and spire rising above the battlements to a height of 120 feet – the reason for its independence from the rest of the church is uncertain. Built almost entirely in the Decorated Gothic style, the main body has been much restored since, including a complete rebuilding of the chancel in 1860. Above a monument in the chancel sits a representation of the devil, an imp said to be more 'impish' than the one at Lincoln Cathedral, the mascot of the county.

3. The road passing by the side of the church is East Gate. Follow this north for 200 yards until, just past the Georgian Manor House, a footpath shoots right and into open fields. Now all eyes are on the impressive outline of Gedney church ahead. A good track follows a ditch, crosses it, and continues along the other side to a hawthorn hedge at the corner of the field. Now cross a bridge and walk on with the ditch on your right. In a few yards branch left onto another track, the church now back in your sights. In ⅓ mile do not miss a green track leaving your route at right-angles. Turn right onto this then left across a small wooden bridge. The path develops with houses on the left and horse paddocks on the right until it enters the trees and negotiates a dog-leg to the right. At a gate the path improves to a lovely grassy lane, then another gate leads you into Rectory Lane. Turn left towards the heart of Gedney and the magnificent church, also dedicated to St Mary Magdalen, is straight in front of you.

The breathtaking church at Gedney is seen at its best, seemingly oversized for a scattered fenland parish, when one is travelling along the A17. Two ranks of huge clear windows line each side of the clerestory, abutting an ashlar-faced tower, tall and elegant. Look to the top of the tower to see the 'little lead spike' standing in for the spire that was planned but never built – the tower would then have looked tall and elegant indeed. The church is otherwise a showcase of architectural details from all periods. The parish register inside bears the marriage banns of a woman with the extraordinary name of Jeflet Banishment Endurance.

4. Turn left onto Church End and the return route is straightforward. Church End leads into Top's Gate, at the end of which the road swings left at a farm shop. From here, just a few hundred yards in front of you, are the tearooms, the end of your journey, and a slice of one of those mouthwatering gateaux!

Walk 5
BOSTON

After the Stump, the most distinctive landmark on the Boston skyline is the colossal Maud Foster Windmill. Here, from Maud's, the superb vegetarian tearoom, you can look out onto the Drain which is also named after Maud Foster, the 16th century owner of this land when the channel was first cut. The Drain is part of engineer John Rennie's ingenious drainage network, which will form the basis of your walk. You begin at the mill, within easy reach of the centre of Boston, a major port in medieval times, now a busy market town boasting fine historic buildings and links with the Pilgrim Fathers. The walk is on good level paths throughout, which become ever more rural as you walk towards the fenland. On only one section of the walk are you not accompanied by the water.

As you enter the Maud Foster Windmill and mount the stairs to Maud's, the tearoom situated on the first floor of the converted mill buildings, the smells of delicious cooking meet you. Apart from the white brick walls, all is wood – the beams on the low ceiling, the floor, the furniture and the banister around the stair well. Here, the food is all first class, all freshly baked, and all suitable for vegetarians. An imaginative menu is chalked onto a wall blackboard, and includes such treats as aubergine Parmagiano, and sweetcorn fritters with a sweet chilli dip. The soups are simply wonderful and there are many mouthwatering cakes on display, including a very tasty vegan rich fruit cake. An assortment of decorative old china cups is matched by the impressive selection of hot beverages, or you might opt for 'real' lemonade. Naturally, only organic flour stoneground by the mill next door is used, and combining your tea with an ascent of the mill is recommended. Opening times are 11 am to 5 pm on Wednesdays and Saturdays (plus Thursdays and Fridays in July and August) and 1 pm to 5 pm on Sundays; also Bank Holidays from 10 am to 5 pm. Telephone: 01205 352188. When Maud's is closed there is a range of alternatives in Boston town centre.

DISTANCE: 4½ miles.
MAPS: OS Landranger 131 Boston and Spalding or Explorer 261 Boston.
STARTING POINT: The Maud Foster Windmill on Willoughly Road in Boston (GR 332447).
HOW TO GET THERE: Leaving Boston town centre on the A16 in the direction of Grimsby you cross Bargate Bridge over Maud Foster Drain and immediately turn left into Willoughby Road. The Maud Foster Windmill cannot be missed on the right and offers limited parking. Further parking is available on the roadside on the opposite side of the Drain.
ALTERNATIVES: You might find it easier to park at Cowbridge, start the walk at the road in point 4 and therefore take your tea at the route's mid-point. You may also wish to take a stroll around the heart of Boston into account.

THE WALK

As well as the largest parish church, Boston can also boast England's tallest working windmill. The seven-storeyed mill was built in 1819 alongside the Drain from which it takes its name. Barges were pulled along the Drain from the River Witham, carrying grinding corn to feed the mill. The tower is constructed of high quality white bricks so impervious that waterproofing the exterior with tar has never been necessary. The five sails, each 37 feet long, stopped turning in 1948, and the mill went into decline until 1987 when restoration began. Today the sails turn on a daily basis – wind permitting – producing the stoneground flours which supply the teashop.

1. Turn right out of the mill courtyard onto Willoughly Road and past a

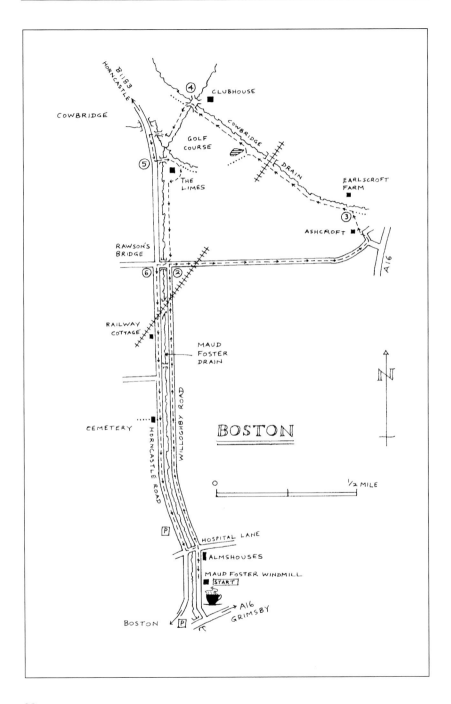

picturesque row of almshouses with Gothic features. The adjacent road is Hospital Lane, which spans Maud Foster Drain by means of an elegant cast-iron footbridge, smartly painted in red and green.

Hospital Lane is not named after the huge modern Pilgrim Hospital but refers to St Leonard's, Boston's former isolation hospital – now vanished. Locals tell a macabre tale of 200 bodies found in unburied lead coffins after the hospital's closure, and of a ghostly figure in a grey coat with the ability to walk through railings!

But you remain on the east bank and continue ahead, looking out for moored barges and fast-moving canoeists on the water below. After a mile a diagonal railway track bridges the Drain and meets the road at a level-crossing. Cross this, and where the Drain goes under a large old brick bridge – Rawson's Bridge – you turn right and once again walk over the railway track.

2. Follow this pleasant residential road for ½ mile until the road turns sharply to the right. At this point leave the road to enter a new housing area on the left, but almost immediately branch left again, passing 'Ashcroft' on your left. Shortly you reach a lovely wide grassy track, onto which you turn left. Below you swans glide gracefully along another wide river, Cowbridge Drain, and beyond Earlscourt Farm on the other bank, you can espy Sibsey Trader Mill in the distance. To your left the view unfolds towards the mill at which you started, and the soaring 'Stump' of St Botolph's.

Boston's importance as a medieval port rivalled that of London, and it was the prosperity generated by the wool trade that funded the construction of St Botolph's church – the Boston Stump. Building began in the early 14th century but the octagonal lantern, which raises the tower to a height of 272 feet, was not completed until 1520. This remains the largest parish church in England, and its 365 steps can be ascended to gain magnificent views over Lincolnshire and The Wash.

3. After ½ mile you meet the railway again. Cross with due care and a little further along, where the path veers left, look out for a stile on your right. Crossing this stile you find yourself on the tenth tee of a golf course next to a dark pool, a remnant of a long-disused canal system. At the far end of this pool are the splendid walls of a brick lock and an iron winch. Your footpath, however, descends to the river immediately after the stile and follows a mown terrace halfway up the high grassy bank. This stretch of Cowbridge Drain has been designated as an important fish breeding ground. Soon the clubhouse is reached at a curious four-way bridge system, where two drainage rivers encounter each other at different levels.

Maud Foster Drain is part of a complex drainage system engineered by John Rennie to channel the water from the fens around Boston away from the land. At Cowbridge two independent tiers of the system intersect, with one drain able to pass underneath the other. Thus the four-way bridge is technically Lincolnshire's only aqueduct. The drains were also used for navigation, and the segment of canal on the golf course was part of the Cowbridge 'aqueduct' bypass. Rennie also designed the two footbridges crossed during the walk, originally a set of three made at Butterley in Derbyshire in 1811.

4. Cross the 'bridge' and turn left to closely follow the water as far as a small clump of trees. Courtesy and attention are required at this point as the true footpath traverses the fairway to join a main road via a concrete bridge and an iron stile. Follow this road back towards Boston until a footbridge, identical to that at Hospital Lane, is reached.

5. The bridge leads you onto a path which almost entirely circles a new house (The Limes) before joining a track to follow Maud Foster Drain back to Rawson's Bridge. This time you cross the bridge and turn left to pursue the opposite bank of the Drain, here covered in lily-pads, and lined with shady trees.

6. One last time over the railway track, look for the disused and dejected Maud Foster Crossing Cottage on your right. Rather more uplifting, ironically, is the delightful cemetery gatehouse ½ mile further along Horncastle Road. This archway leads towards an avenue of enormous trees, with further avenues leading off to various chapels and towers. Laid out in 1845, these grounds have become home to many species of plants and birds. From the gatehouse superb views of the windmill accompany you back to the bridge and over the Drain to Maud's.

Walk 6
WAINFLEET-ALL-SAINTS

This walk is based upon a village which just missed out on being one of the country's most important ports. Wainfleet-All-Saints, once on the coast, was a thriving medieval port, but eventually its harbour lost the continual battle against silting and the sea receded. The walk follows the banks of the River Steeping into the heart of the open fens as far back as the Middle Ages and the long-vanished town of Wainfleet St Mary's. Here the route passes through a spectacularly sited churchyard before continuing along a breezy field path to make its way back to the splendid museum building in Wainfleet.

No other village in England can boast a library such as this! The red-brick Magdalen College stands majestic in the sleepy Lincolnshire countryside. Above the library is a fascinating museum containing local nuggets ranging from a 3,000 year old axe-head to the nose cone of the only bomb to hit Wainfleet. The teashop is simple but too delightful not to include. Until recently teas were served in the small reading room next to the museum, reached via a spiral stone stairway. Now rehoused in a tiny glass-topped courtyard flanked by a Victorian kitchen, the tables in the teashop spill out into a small walled garden, neat flower beds brimming with every herb imaginable. Teas, coffees and soft drinks are served by enthusiastic volunteers, who will be happy to chat to you about this glorious building. Scones and cakes are also on offer, and in summer, a limited range of light snacks. The teashop is open from Easter to September between 1.30 pm and 4.30 pm, but is closed on Mondays (except bank holidays) and Wednesdays. Telephone: 01754 880343. Wainfleet offers a selection of alternative places selling food and drink if the teashop is closed.

DISTANCE: 4½ miles.
MAPS: OS Landranger 122 (Skegness) or Explorer 261 (Boston).
STARTING POINT: Magdalen College in Wainfleet-All-Saints (GR 499588).
HOW TO GET THERE: The A52 bypasses Wainfleet on its way along the coast between Skegness and Boston, and roads lead into the village from both directions. From the south approach, cross the railway and turn first right into Silver Street, where Magdalen College stands in front of you. Some parking is available, or you can park in the nearby streets.
ALTERNATIVES: The walk could be started from almost any point along its route, but please allow time to fully explore the sights of Wainfleet.

THE WALK
In 1484 the illustrious William Patten of Waynflete, then Bishop of Winchester, decided to found a free college in his home town to reflect his other foundation, Magdalen College in Oxford, and Tattershall Castle, on which he had also worked. What he erected is the remarkable brick hall (one of the first in Lincolnshire) of Magdalen College, flanked by its pair of enormous octagonal turrets. It continued in service until 1933, when a new grammar school at Skegness led to its closure as a school.

1. From the museum walk along Silver Street to the High Street and cross the railway line to your left. Look for a signed footpath (Church Walk) after the next road on your right which takes you past new houses and into the 'Great Field' – actually allotment gardens. The once-metalled path leads straight across them via two footbridges. After ½ mile turn left onto a road, then right onto another footpath, taking care to keep the ditch on your right. Past a scrubby vegetable patch, you cross a road and climb the high levee of the River Steeping.

2. Now follow this bank to the right for ½ mile, enjoying glorious views

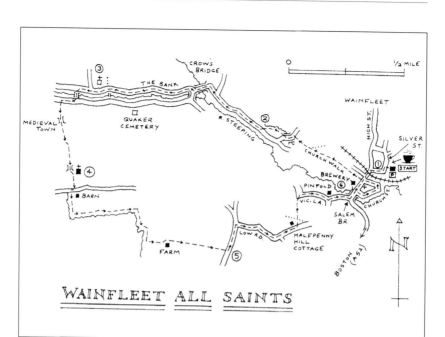

WAINFLEET ALL SAINTS

to the Lincolnshire Wolds, until you reach the impressive brick Crow's Bridge. Cross this and turn immediately right into Wainfleet Bank, with the course of the original river on your left, and follow the road to the site of an ancient church and graveyard on your right.

This churchyard contained the original church of All Saints, which in 1718 proudly received a new central tower complete with bells. The weight of these additions, however, proved too heavy, and the church was declared unsafe for worship. In 1820 it was demolished and replaced by the current building in the village centre, using much of the old stone and several other features. The 15th century memorial to Richard Patten, father of William of Waynflete, stood in the south transept of the old building.

Just across the old river from here is another religious relic – a Quaker burial ground dating from 1691. Graves were unmarked in keeping with Quaker belief, and included that of William Reckitt, a missionary to America and the West Indies, who died in 1769.

3. A short way past the site of the church spot a footbridge crossing the stream to your left. Having crossed this continue in the same direction to find a footpath sign at a stile on your left. Follow the path over fields criss-crossed with earthworks belonging to the medieval town of Wainfleet. Cross a bridge guarded by two stiles beyond which the way runs alongside a hedge lit bright red in autumn by rosehips and hawthorn berries. Another bridge then leads you into the enchanting isolated churchyard of St Mary's, a large church set in a small wood, a lone survivor of the deserted medieval settlement.

4. Leave the churchyard through an arched aisle of overhead tree branches and an ornate carved lychgate to reach Church Lane. Opposite you here is a small cheerful barn and, to its right, an opening onto a good field track. This track, though winding, is simple to follow and a mile later, having improved to a tarmac lane, comes to a junction.

5. Turn left here, then right into Low road, until you spot Halfpenny Hill Cottage on your left – take the footpath just past here. Over a track, past a field, and along a shaded passage, you find yourself in Vicarage Lane, and you head right to rejoin Low Road where the River Steeping comes alongside at the old Pinfold – the pound for stray cattle. Left over Salem Bridge you next pass Bateman's Brewery, centred around the tall ivy-clad windmill tower, topped by a beer-bottle weathervane.

The beginnings of the brewery are unusual indeed. In 1874 George Bateman, a farmer himself, rented a brewery in Wainfleet in order to provide 'refreshment' – delivered by dray – for other farmers and farmworkers. The farmers, however, were only obliged to settle their brewery bills at the local fair, held twice annually – and then in kind not cash. There then followed a huge feast at the brewery, a tradition observed until 1930. Progress from these humble origins has been spectacular. The brewery has continued to expand and now occupies a whole group of 19th century industrial buildings, including the castellated windmill, adopted as the brewery symbol.

6. Behind the buildings on the other side of the street from the brewery runs Church Street. This delightful riverside lane can be joined at Salem Bridge and makes a worthwhile addition to the route. It rejoins the High Street at the parish church of All Saints, with its curious lead-capped bell-tower. From here a simple stroll over the railway line takes you back to Silver Street on your right, and Magdalen College. Now, as you relax with a reviving cup of tea, time to chat about your expedition to the friendly volunteers.

Walk 7
HECKINGTON

A short, simple stroll around a small town – or is it a large village? Heckington is still a picturesque place and contains a number of remarkable traditional brick buildings. The former Pearoom is one of these and now houses the area's finest art and crafts complex. Here you are invited to take a delicious lunch or tea in the rustic surroundings of the teashop. The level walking is all on good paved surfaces, and the climax of the tour is a visit to one of England's most splendid Decorated churches.

 The second floor of Heckington's Pearoom, sited in the actual chamber formerly used for sorting peas and beans, is where you will find the tearoom. Here the original wooden beams and struts remain in place, with wooden furniture and simple crockery and cutlery completing the 'rural mill' flavour. Workshops for various creative activities lead off to all sides, art books and magazines lie everywhere, and the atmosphere is relaxed and unassuming. Everything has been baked in-house –

everything that is except the delicious 'oaties', which are imported from Derbyshire. These are hand-made oatcake pancake rolls stuffed with your choice from the imaginative savoury fillings. The rest of the menu is mainly vegetarian, and a daily 'vegetarian special' is always available. But it is the quiches and cakes that steal the show. The marble cake and the banana and walnut are tasty enough, but the chocolate cake is superb. The Pearoom is open from 10 am to 5 pm between Tuesday and Saturday, on Mondays in season, and from noon on Sundays. Telephone: 01529 460765. If the Pearoom is closed there are inns serving food in the village, while the town of Sleaford is just 5 miles to the west.

DISTANCE: 1½ miles.

MAPS: OS Landranger 130 (Grantham) or Explorer 261 (Boston).

STARTING POINT: The Pearoom in Heckington (GR 147437).

HOW TO GET THERE: The busy A17 from Boston to Sleaford now bypasses Heckington and link roads lead you into the town from both directions. From the town centre turn south onto the B1394 and the Pearoom is on your left just before the level crossing. Parking is available here.

ALTERNATIVES: Park in the centre of Heckington and explore the town before walking out to the Pearoom. For those who need to stretch their limbs in search of more rural surroundings, stride towards nearby Asgarby – easily found on the OS map, north-west of Heckington.

THE WALK

The 1890 Pearoom is really part of the nearby railway complex, and was used as a pea-sorting warehouse until as recently as 1962, fed by its own branch line. Restored since 1980 this wonderful old relic of the farming industry now houses a contemporary craft gallery, two exhibition areas, a range of working and educational workshops, a tearoom and, of course, a detailed account of the history of 'pea-riddling'!

1. From the Pearoom head along Station Road away from the railway to enter New Street on your left. The terrace of houses on your right was raised by one John Pocklington purely to spoil the view from the nearby garden of the doctor who had committed Pocklington to an asylum. Mad? Him? A short footpath leads you from New Street into Banks Lane to pass the Diamond Jubilee Cottages on your left, the former site of Heckington Hall.

2. On reaching the village green admire a well-proportioned row of Victorian almshouses, and its neighbour, the Nag's Head Inn – did Dick

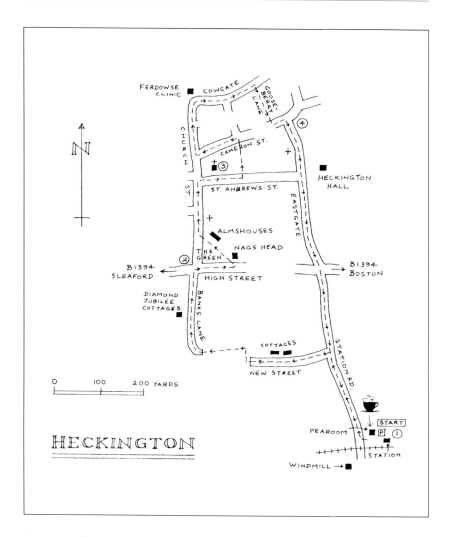

FERDOWSE CLINIC
COWGATE
GOOSEBERRY LANE
CHURCH ST
CAMERON ST.
③
ST. ANDREWS ST.
EASTGATE
HECKINGTON HALL
ALMSHOUSES
THE GREEN
②
NAG'S HEAD
B1394 SLEAFORD
HIGH STREET
B1394 BOSTON
DIAMOND JUBILEE COTTAGES
BANKS LANE
COTTAGES
NEW STREET
STATION RD
0   100   200 YARDS
PEAROOM
START
P ①
STATION
WINDMILL →

HECKINGTON

Turpin really stay here? But all eyes are now on the jewel ahead, the splendid tower of St Andrew's parish church.

St Andrew's ranks as one of Lincolnshire's most glorious churches, as complete an example of Decorated Gothic architecture as can be found. Begun by the Abbots of Bardney, the present building in its cruciform state dates from 1305, and has become known as the 'Cathedral of the Fens'. Outside, a wealth of splendid gargoyles and elaborate window tracery lead your eye to the top of a pinnacled tower, crowned by a magnificent spire. Inside, the renowned detailed carving of the Easter Sepulchre is not bettered anywhere in the country.

3. To enjoy a tour of the church's exterior walk first into St Andrew's Street, then along a tree-lined path at the rear of the churchyard and back along Cameron Street. Turn right onto Church Street once more and, where you swing into Cowgate, sneak a look at a magnificent ivy-clad building on the left – nowadays a clinic. Passing further attractive cottages, continue until you spot Gooseberry Lane on your right. This passage returns you to Cameron Street, where a swift left-right brings you into Eastgate.

4. The current Heckington Hall can now be espied above the imposing high brick walls. The Hall is the former home of William Little, who in the 19th century founded the *London News*, patented a series of wall tiles and invented a successful sheep-dip! Inspired by this Victorian vigour, you now stride the length of Eastgate and Station Road, drawn by a superb view of the windmill, and the promise of something a bit special in the Pearoom!

If the church is Heckington's brightest jewel then the three 19th century industrial gems set in a cluster around the railway line run it a close second. The Pearoom, naturally, is one of these. The windmill, the only surviving eight-sailed mill in the country, is another, still wind powered today, still grinding corn. Originally built with only five sails in 1830, it was not until they were destroyed in an 1890 thunderstorm that the mill received eight new sails, bought from the redundant Tuxford Mill at Skirbeck near Boston. As with other Lincolnshire mills, Heckington was left to decay for much of the last century, until being restored to full working order in 1986. Finally there are the station buildings and signal-box, dating from 1859 and little changed since. This is a working station and Heckington's Village Trust have reopened the former First Class waiting room as a small museum, while the level crossing gates are still operated by a real person!

Walk 8
FOLKINGHAM

From Folkingham most walking guides shepherd their readers west along a well-trodden path towards Walcot, Newton and Pickworth. You, however, are heading in the opposite direction along quieter paths and peaceful lanes to the most silent place of all – Sempringham. Here the tranquil atmosphere and solitude of the noble medieval church are matched only by the remarkable tale of the priory that once flourished nearby. All this is in sharp contrast to the showpiece village of Folkingham itself – a handsome Georgian market square, a towering 16-pinnacled church, and the real highlight of the day's walking, the Old Reading Room. This is now a coffee shop with the most enviable reputation for friendly service, stylish surroundings and, above all, first class food.

Every so often you come across a teashop which stands out from the rest, and the Old Reading Room Coffee Shop in Folkingham, built of honey-coloured stone in the 16th century, may be deemed the flagship of Lincolnshire teashops. Where to start? Maybe its perfect location at the head of this fine market place, church towering behind, historic coaching inn next door. As you enter you are shown into one of two comfortable rooms with low beamed ceilings. This was a lending library until the turn of the century so books are everywhere, and a stone ingle at one end overflows with antiques and memorabilia. Though always busy, the Old Reading Room manages to maintain a relaxed atmosphere.

Hot pancakes covered in cheese sauce with various savoury fillings, including Smoked Fish Florentine, are the speciality, but everything here is special – even the tripe and onions! They don't hold back with the puddings either. The Summer Berry Surprise boasts of 'a kick in the bottom' while the Banoffee Pie simple declares itself 'wickedly delicious' – neither is exaggerating. You will not need telling that everything is freshly baked. This wonderful establishment is open every day except Mondays and Tuesdays, from 10.30 am to 5.30 pm (3 pm on Sundays). Telephone: 01529 497377. The Greyhound Inn next door – also an antiques centre – serves meals if the Old Reading Room is not open.

DISTANCE: 7½ miles.

MAPS: OS Landranger 130 (Grantham) or Explorer 248 (Bourne and Heckington).

STARTING POINT: The Old Reading Room Coffee Shop in Folkingham (GR 072337).

HOW TO GET THERE: Folkingham is situated midway between Sleaford and Bourne on the A15. There is ample parking around the Market Square, at the top of which stands the Old Reading Room.

ALTERNATIVES: Park at the church at Sempringham (reached from the B1177) and walk to Folkingham for tea at the mid-point of the walk.

THE WALK

1. Folkingham's long Market Square tumbles gently down the hillside, ever narrower as it passes splendid buildings on both sides, some brick, some stone, the Manor House on the left deserving special examination. Just before a petrol station at the bottom of the hill a footpath leads you to the left (look for the yellow arrow) and over a track to a stile. Now on the site of the former castle, you skirt the wooden banks in the centre of the grounds and exit next to the austere House of Correction.

Folkingham's importance was not only as a coaching station along the London road, but also as the seat of the Quarter Sessions Court, and in 1825 a new prison was built on the site of the medieval castle to accommodate offenders. Treats in store for the inmates of the 'House of Correction' included a treadwheel, a whipping-post and a hand-crank.

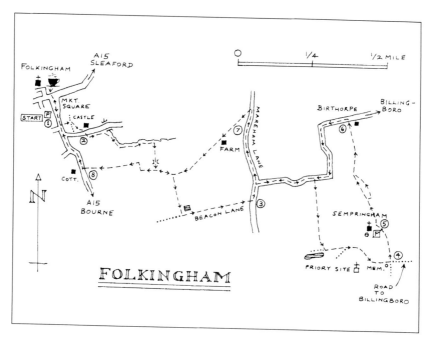

FOLKINGHAM

2. Over the road a path leads into a field and left along the hedge. At a new brick bridge this path bears right to follow a winding stream. In ½ mile you are directed right, up the hillside beside a small ditch, to a footbridge, which you cross. Now walk left on a good farm track as far as a junction at an open courtyard. Turn right here, up the hill once more, and left when you reach the summit, onto Beacon Lane. This high-level track leads you to Mareham Lane, an old Roman route.

3. At this road the OS map declares a right of way across the field in front of you. However, due to its complete obliteration and the 'Dog-Wires' warnings, this path is rendered totally unrecommendable – especially to dogs! Instead a left-right movement takes you onto a lane lined with young oak trees. Before this lane bends left, a clear track shoots off to the right with a hedge alongside. Follow this track all the way to the bottom of the hill. At the end of this grassy trail turn left onto another track and follow this until you come across a stone tablet on your right.

The memorial stone tells the melancholy tale of Princess Gwenllian, daughter of the Prince of Wales and granddaughter of Simon de Montfort. Totally unwanted, she was 'imprisoned' in the nunnery at Sempringham

41

at the tender age of seventeen months, and remained confined until she died here 54 years later, in 1337.

4. Now walk along the short road to Sempringham's parish church of St Andrew.

Of all the Lincolnshire churches which stand in splendid isolation, St Andrew's has to be the most utterly alone – a parish church whose parish has completely disappeared. Only a handful of yew trees keep it company, and even the best approach is by way of a track across open fields.

This solitude did not always prevail. In the 12th century, a monastery was founded here by Gilbert of Sempringham, inhabited by the white-coated Gilbertine monks, the only wholly British monastic order. Among their number was Robert de Brunne, whose wooden effigy – 30 feet high – can be found amongst the sculptures in Bourne Wood (see Walk 2). The monastery was unique in that it also admitted women. Though born crippled, Gilbert lived to be 106, and when he was canonized after his death, the monastery assumed greater importance, and expanded accordingly - a huge number of monks and nuns dwelt here at its height. St Andrew's church was assumed to be built around the monastery's nave until excavations slightly to the south revealed its true location in 1939.

5. Out of the churchyard gates turn left along the perimeter wall and continue to a footbridge. The next field is best followed by means of the curving ditch to your right, and, reaching a lonely signpost, you head right towards the crest of the hill, and then for the left-hand edge of the farm buildings coming into view.

6. Turn left onto the road at Birthorpe and follow it left and right as far back as Mareham Lane. Now turn right and, in ½ mile, look for a muddy lane heading left towards an attractive group of derelict red-brick farm buildings and a huge wine goblet of a water tower in the distance.

7. Simply pursue this track for 1½ miles, taking in the superb views of the nearby villages, until you reach the main road at a small blue and white cottage.

8. Folkingham is now just a short walk along the road to your right, but caution must be exercised on this brief pathless stretch. Soon you enter the Market Square once again, with the sanctuary of the Old Reading Room at the top of the hill in front of you.

Walk 9
FULBECK

This walk includes not only an excellent teashop, but a group of craft workshops and the elegant Fulbeck Hall. The route links two stone-built villages along the Lincoln Cliff, offering spectacular views over the Trent Valley to Newark. Fulbeck and Caythorpe are beautiful villages, and both reward a full exploration. Both have a church of distinction, though differing vastly from each other – as do their respective Halls, Fulbeck imposing and accessible, Caythorpe hidden and mysterious.

The former stables of Fulbeck Manor have been skilfully converted into a series of thriving craft workshops, but the most charming is the old tack room, which now houses a small, friendly teashop. Here the menu of light meals is centred around the speciality toasted rarebits – a dozen variations are offered, including the chicken and bacon stack and the 'Scottish Treat' (smoked salmon). 'Prawn Perfection' and 'Farmer's Friend' (cheeses and relishes) are among the choice of excellent open sandwiches, and the chef's daily specials are displayed on a board. In good weather you can exchange the intimacy of the interior for the sunny courtyard, a fine setting for your afternoon tea – you will not want to miss out on the scrummy cakes displayed. At the end of your meal you can wander directly into the adjoining gift showrooms and the workshops of the local craftspeople, among them a blacksmith, a clockmaker and a rocking horse specialist. The Manor Stables Tea Rooms are open (apart from the Christmas and New Year period) between 10.30 am and 4.30 pm every day from Tuesday to Sunday; open on Bank Holiday Mondays. Telephone: 01400 273724. When the teashop is closed refreshments are available at the Hare and Hounds nearby.

DISTANCE: 3½ miles.

MAPS: OS Landranger 121 (Lincoln) and 130 (Grantham) or Explorer 272 (Lincoln and Sleaford).

STARTING POINT: The Manor Stables Craft Workshops Tea Rooms in Fulbeck (GR 948503).

HOW TO GET THERE: Fulbeck is found on the Lincoln to Grantham road (A607) one mile south of Leadenham. Approaching Fulbeck from Leadenham the Manor Stables are on your right past the church. Parking is limited – please park at the sports field on the opposite side of the main road.

ALTERNATIVES: Start the walk from the church at Caythorpe – the teashop then features in the middle of the walk. The superfit will find Stragglethorpe Hall (3 miles west) a rewarding but distant addition to the itinerary.

THE WALK

1. Leaving the stable courtyard turn left onto the main road and left again into Rectory Lane, alongside the long wall of the Hare and Hounds. At the end of this wall you are greeted by a truly glorious English village setting. In front of you a square stretches across a green to the church set in the trees behind.

Turn left into High Street, continue straight ahead to a stream and climb Sudthorpe Hill, enjoying an unbeatable view back to Fulbeck on your right. In Sudthorpe the footpath leads you between the houses and into a field.

2. Follow a vague track heading for the far right-hand corner, and, when all seems lost, spot your path dipping below a large tree near a telegraph pole to emerge on a clearer path around a field edge. Turn left along here, then right when you reach a farm track. This track develops into a grassy lane, and you follow it straight to a footpath sign on your left, beneath a row of elm trees.

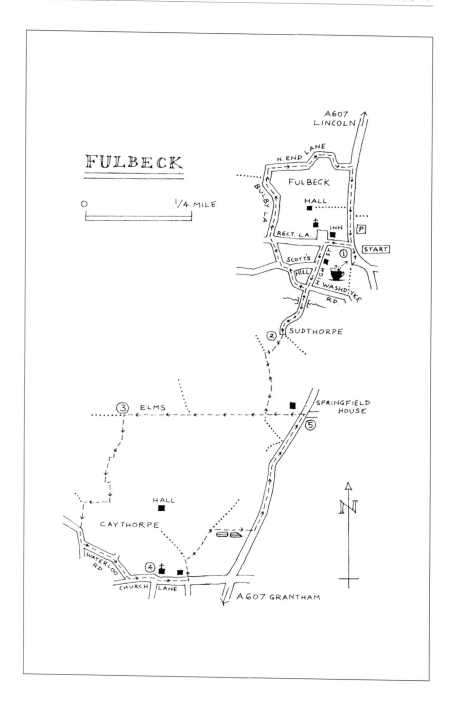

FULBECK

0   1/4 MILE

A607
LINCOLN

N. END LANE

FULBECK

BULBY LA.

HALL

RECT. LA.

INN

P

START

SCOTT'S

HILL

HIGH ST

①

WASHDYKE RD.

SUDTHORPE

②

③ ELMS

SPRINGFIELD HOUSE

⑤

HALL

CAYTHORPE

N

WATERLOO RD.

④

CHURCH LANE

A607 GRANTHAM

3. Head through the fields along this path, and when it reaches a hedge keep this to your left. Do not be tempted by a stile, but continue around the edge of the fields, until you find yourself on a road at the edge of Caythorpe. Turn left onto Waterloo Road, and left again when you reach Church Lane, checking out a curious white dovecote on top of a nearby barn. Church Lane leads you, understandably, to St Vincent's church.

The church at Caythorpe is remarkable for a number of reasons. Firstly, this is one of only five British churches dedicated to St Vincent – not surprising, as he was a 4th century martyr who lived and worked in Spain. Secondly, the nave is almost unique in that it is split into two by a lofty arcade of slender octagonal pillars, running end to end. Finally, the exterior stone work is laid in alternate light and dark bands of ironstone and Ancaster stone. Above the elegant central tower rises a tall spire – this was rebuilt in 1860 after being struck by lightning.

4. Beyond the church pass between two imposing stone pillars into the entrance drive to Caythorpe Hall. In a few yards you hurdle a stile on your right and cross the parkland to a second stile. Beyond this the true path observes a diagonal course but is unclear, and you will prefer to skirt two ponds on your right to reach the road. Now stride left, accompanied by a decaying stone wall, evidence of the past riches in Caythorpe.

5. Turn left onto the lane at Springfield House and, reaching the footpath on the right once more, simply retrace your route back into Fulbeck.

A circuit around the lanes in the village should not be omitted. Washdyke Road, Scott's Hill or Rectory Lane will lead you to Bulby Lane, which in turn takes you to North End Lane. Return on the main road, passing the Hall, the church and the inn on your way back to the Tea Rooms, that toasted rarebit and those scones.

Fine wrought-iron gates open onto an avenue of great lime trees leading to Fulbeck Hall, rebuilt in 1733 in the 'Stamfordian' style, after a fire had destroyed most of the earlier work. The Hall has been in the hands of the Fane family since well before the fire, and their treasures grace every room. Perhaps the most interesting room, however, is the 'Map Room'. In 1944 Fulbeck Hall was commandeered as the headquarters of the 1st Airborne Division, and it was here that battle plans for the fateful mission to Arnhem were laid. The Map Room has since been restored to its 1944 condition and houses an exhibition open to the public.

Walk 10
NETTLEHAM

The village of Nettleham near Lincoln is a perfectly preserved collection of mellow stone cottages, shops and inns built alongside a pretty, sparkling stream. The village church is at its hub, and ducks congregate around the bridge where the trees in the churchyard form shady archways over the pathway and the water. Your short village ramble follows the stream past an old mill in one direction, and extends to a lovely teashop next to the triangular village green in the other, where you can indulge yourself with a clotted cream tea!

If you stand under the trees on The Green and look across East Street you will notice a stone building newer than most around you. This is the Tea Cosy, a small, lively tearoom where passers-by and locals mix to create a cheerful atmosphere. The Tea Cosy prides itself on friendly service and first class food – all home-baked. A traditional menu is supplemented by daily special dishes, and a choice of two excellent soups. Delicious sandwiches include early morning bacon and mushroom, while a later treat offers you one of Lincolnshire's rare opportunities to take afternoon tea with real clotted cream! Other puddings and cakes taste as wonderful as they look – try the Bailey's cheesecake – everything attractively presented on white china. Finishing touches include sugar tongs and beaded lace covers on the sugar bowls. The Tea Cosy is open from 10 am to 5 pm on Tuesdays to Saturdays, plus Mondays from May to September. Telephone: 01522 751077. There are inns around the village serving food if the Tea Cosy is closed.

DISTANCE: 1½ miles.

MAPS: OS Landranger 121 (Lincoln) or Explorer 272 (Lincoln and Sleaford).

STARTING POINT: The Tea Cosy on The Green in Nettleham (GR 009754).

HOW TO GET THERE: Leave Lincoln on the A46 towards Market Rasen and a
   mile past the ring-road roundabout take the right-hand turn signed for
   Nettleham. At the village church turn left into Church Street. This leads you to
   The Green and the Tea Cosy. There is plenty of roadside parking.

ALTERNATIVES: Those needing a sterner test of their walking skills might
   continue past the lake and over the A46 to explore Riseholme and the
   surrounding area.

THE WALK

1. Facing The Green outside the teashop turn right along East Street then right again into The Crescent. Battles House on the corner incorporates an old butcher's shop and is one of several buildings around the village which began life as a farmhouse. The Crescent leads you back into East Street. Return as far as Cross Street on the right, follow this as far as the Black Horse Inn, then turn left to re-enter The Green. Now branch right into Church Street, passing a 17th century cottage on your left (now a shop), to arrive at the impressive village church, which should be thoroughly explored, inside and out.

The origins of All Saints are Saxon, but the church was mainly built in the 13th century in the Early English style. It was extended in Victorian times and much changed again after a fire in the east end in 1969 – as you stand inside the church today, the cool modern white of the renovated chancel contrasts with the warm colours of the ancient nave. Stained-glass set in a lancet window depicts William Patten (see Walk 6) and outside can be found the gravestone of a poor 19 year old post-boy, gruesomely murdered in 1732 by the Hallam brothers. The Hallams were caught, found guilty of this and another murder only the previous night and subsequently hanged in irons.

2. Cross Jubilee Bridge over the gurgling Nettleham Beck and turn right into the High Street. The cottages on your left are 300 years old, while on your right you can spot a notable Venetian window above the entrance to the White Hart, as you approach the site of the medieval Bishop's Palace just past the Methodist church.

The once extensive buildings of Nettleham Manor have now all but vanished. First built in 1086 the Manor became the Bishop of Lincoln's Palace in 1101, on the direction of Henry I. This would have been a large country house built around a fine long banqueting hall, and protected by ditches and high walls. A gatehouse led into the grounds, where a chapel, stables and a farmstead also stood.

In 1301 Edward I arrived as the guest of Bishop Alderley, and here declared his son to be the first Prince of Wales. The palace was badly damaged during the Louth uprising of 1536, but remained in use for another 50 years. Legend has it that the old palace was linked to Lincoln Cathedral by an underground passage, but as the two are nearly four miles apart this seems preposterous. In the early 18th century the palace was demolished and the stone used to rebuild the new Bishop's Palace next to the cathedral in Lincoln.

3. Cross into Watermill Lane, which leads you down to the ford and the attractive Watermill House. Originally the most important of seven mills in the village this has undergone extensive rebuilding. A path leads over the water and past the door of the mill. Continue up the lane on the other side for a few yards before joining a footpath on the left which follows the wooded bank of the stream until it opens out onto grass alongside a tranquil lake.

4. The return route is straightforward and rewarding. Simply retrace your steps to the mill then continue along Beckside to Jubilee Bridge once again, passing several more charming cottages, Vicar's Wood and the gate into the churchyard. Beyond the bridge the brookside path continues on the opposite bank, now quiet and shaded by tall trees, until it emerges in Vicarage Lane.

5. Turn left and pass Beck House on your right, built in the 16th century but sadly no longer thatched. You are now back at The Green, with the possibility of a large slice of coffee and walnut cake waiting to welcome you inside the Tea Cosy.

Walk 11
FALDINGWORTH

This, as they say, is a walk of two halves. Part one is a comfortable stroll along peaceful country lanes, visiting a redundant church which is home to two very important residents, and admiring the views to the Wolds in the east and the cathedral at Lincoln in the opposite direction. The second half gives you the opportunity to earn your treat at Brownlow's teashop, as a muddy woodland track leads on to a series of field footpaths. Don't forget that in summer Faldingworth plays host to a large number of highly unusual guests, but more about them further on . . .

Most Lincolnshire folk remember the Brownlow Antiques Centre as a public house, but it was originally built as part of Lord Brownlow's farm. Don't let it put you off, but the converted barn which now houses the charming Brownlow's teashop, used to be home to a number of pigs, with the Skegness donkeys joining them for the winter. Considerably cleaner these days, the atmosphere of a rustic barn is maintained, with roof beams and farm cottage furniture. Alternatively, you can sit in the sheltered courtyard among the antiques from next door. Hot and cold light meals and sandwiches are served, plus scrummy scones and cakes from a Market Rasen baker – one of the best in Lincolnshire! Choose from a selection of teas and coffees with your food, or finish with that ice-cream sundae you were trying to say 'no' to. Brownlow's is open all week except Monday, 10 am to 5 pm (Sundays 12 noon to 5 pm). It does, however, close for the winter, and you should phone 01673 885367 to check. If you do not find the teashop open the Coach and Horses in the village also serves good food.

DISTANCE: 6 miles.
MAPS: OS Landranger 121 (Lincoln) or Explorer 272 (Lincoln and Sleaford).
STARTING POINT: The Brownlow Antiques Centre in Faldingworth (GR 067847).
HOW TO GET THERE: From Lincoln take the A46 in the direction of Market Rasen and after 10 miles you reach the village of Faldingworth. The Brownlow Antiques Centre is prominent on your left with the teashop and car park just behind. There is also roadside parking around the village.
ALTERNATIVES: Buslingthorpe (point 2) and Freisthorpe (point 5) would both make good alternative starting points for the walk.

THE WALK

1. From Brownlow's walk left along the main road towards Market Rasen. At the end of the village where the main road curves left you branch right onto Buslingthorpe Road, which is in fact a quiet, pleasant lane. In less than a mile you reach the farming hamlet of Buslingthorpe, with the cream brick tower of the church vividly outlined against the tall dark trees behind.

Pleasing but unassuming outside, St Michael's church holds treasures within. One is a stone tomb-chest bearing a life-sized effigy of the knight Sir John de Buslingthorpe. Sir John's pillow is supported by two kneeling angels and his feet rest on a lion. The other is a famous military brass to Sir Richard de Buslingthorpe, set in a Purbeck marble coffin lid. This, like the effigy, dates from around 1340, making it one of the earliest surviving brasses in the country. The church was declared redundant in 1984 and is now maintained by the Churches Conservation Trust.

2. Back onto the lane past the church, inspect the moat in the grounds of the 18th century manor house. Continue until the road pivots to the right beyond Manor Farm, with substantial earthworks from the medieval village in the fields to your right. In another 200 yards the road turns

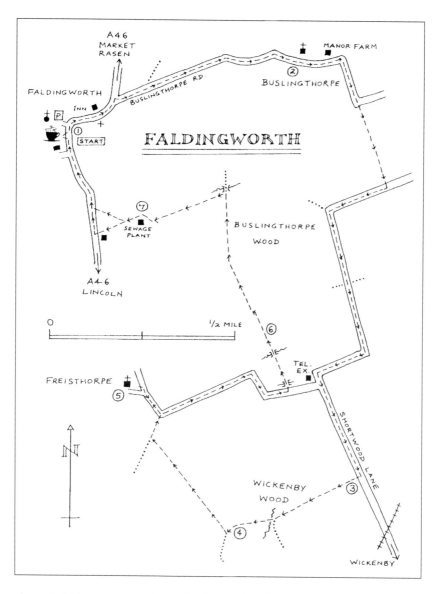

sharp left, but you continue dead straight ahead on a limestone track, which leads you over a hill and onto another lane. Turning right you follow this winding road for a full mile, passing Buslingthorpe Wood on your right. Bear left at a tiny telephone exchange and, after ⅓ mile, look out for an entrance into Wickenby Wood Nature Reserve on the right.

3. Once into this wood the terrain changes dramatically, and as you trudge along the muddy track you will feel that you are earning your indulgence at the teashop! Remain alert, though, as you encounter an abundance of trees and plantlife, birds and small animals. Where the trail bears left look carefully for a small ditch to your right, on the other side of which a lesser path leads towards daylight ahead.

4. Now clear of the wood, follow the edge of this large field to the left, until a clear path on the right doubles back sharply through the field. Straight and true, this long path takes you to a farm track, which in turn leads to the road in the village of Freisthorpe, with St Peter's church standing a short distance to your left.

Each year in June Freisthorpe and Faldingworth are invaded by a group of unnerving characters – humorous, magical and a little bit frightening – the scarecrows! Lurking around every corner, these extraordinary creations, made with skill and flair to a very high standard by the villagers and linked annually by a common theme, take over the two villages. They reappear for an encore in late July then vanish until the next summer. For details, telephone: 01673 885807.

5. Having surveyed the church, about-turn and follow the lane back. The road crooks right and left, until, spotting a small footbridge on your left, you cross and pursue a path beside a ditch as far as a forbidding hedge. Puzzled at first, peer behind this hedge to locate a tiny wooden bridge over the next ditch and into another field.

6. Do not opt to follow the perimeter of this field as you may disturb sensitive pheasant breeding grounds. Instead, pick as careful a way as possible over the field, targeting the left-hand corner of Buslingthorpe Wood ahead of you. Keeping the wood on your right, progress along the footpath which dives through a gap in a hedge before becoming broader along the edge of the next enclosure. (The OS map shows a footpath going diagonally across these fields, but none exists.) Eventually reaching a concrete bridge, turn left in front of it and walk on to pass a small water treatment plant on the left.

7. The true path now crosses a small field on your right, but you might prefer to walk around the edge of this field, or even continue along the firm track as far as the main road. Either way only ¼ mile along this road lie Faldingworth and Brownlow's, and your well-deserved treat.

Walk 12
WOODHALL SPA

Woodhall Spa, originally an Edwardian spa resort, is an ideal place to simply wander around and enjoy, so this walk can be adapted to suit your needs, or joined anywhere along its route – whichever way you approach it you are going to like this relaxed town. Everything is set in magnificent woodland, notably pine, birch and colourful rhododendrons. The spa is no more but you will find charming reminders of its heyday, like the Kinema in the Woods, one of the country's few back-projection cinemas, which can even offer entertainment on an original Compton organ. When your walking has given you an appetite, Just Desserts, a delightful coffee shop, is an excellent place to relax.

When the owner of a small Woodhall garage decided to call it a day in 1998, his daughter soon reopened the premises – but this time as an Ice Cream Parlour and Coffee Shop, Just Desserts – giving a bright new lease of life to the old building on the Broadway. Outside, the original petrol pumps and distinctive garage frontage tell the story, while the interior is smartly furnished in pine, with potted plants and china teacups completing the picture. The expected selection of meals is on offer, but you may like to try something a little more unusual. Maybe a mouthwatering 'Dorset savoury' – a toasted sandwich filled with cheddar cheese and apple. But it is when you move to the dessert course that the choice becomes impossible. The sundaes are made with top quality local ice-cream, and toffee or cherry are just two of the pancake fillings. How about a hot toasted sandwich with honey and walnut, or even banana, chocolate and maple? And there are some marvellous home-made scones and cakes to enjoy at teatime. Telephone: 01526 352445. Just Desserts is open every day from 10 am to about 5 pm, but if closed Woodhall has plenty of alternatives to offer.

DISTANCE: 2½ miles.
MAPS: OS Landranger 122 (Skegness) or Explorer 273 (Lincolnshire Wolds South).
STARTING POINT: Just Desserts on the Broadway in Woodhall Spa (GR 196632).
HOW TO GET THERE: Entering Woodhall on the Broadway – the B1191 from Horncastle – you will see Just Desserts on your right just past an old chapel on the corner of Iddesleigh Road. Park on the main road or any of the adjoining side streets.
ALTERNATIVES: The walk can be made more demanding by extending it as far as Kirkstead to visit the abbey ruins and St Leonard's church.

THE WALK

1. From the teashop door turn right towards the town centre, and walk as far as Royal Square.

In Royal Square stands a monument to the members of 617 Squadron – the 'Dambusters'. In 1943 their Officers' Mess became established in Woodhall's Petwood Hotel. 617 Squadron's finest hour came with the successful raid on six Ruhr dams in Germany's industrial heartland. The attack was led by Wing Commander Guy Gibson, who later received the Victoria Cross. But the price of the mission was high, with 8 of the 19 bombers and 53 of the 133 crew failing to return. The memorial, in the shape of a dam, stands on the site of the Royal Hotel, itself destroyed by bombing in 1943.

At Royal Square turn right along Stixwould Road, shaded by the huge trees in the graveyard opposite. When you come to Coronation Road on your right follow this through the pine woods, and after a short distance the road broadens into a clearing where two colossal redwood trees tower above all else. You are now facing the Kinema in the Woods, which is still thriving today, and the deserted spa, which is not.

John Parkinson had three dreams. To build a city, to plant a forest and to sink a mine. But his plans went horribly wrong, and in 1826 at the age of 54 he was declared bankrupt. His 'city' was New Bolingbroke, with little more than its noble crescent to show, his forests had to be sold – Ostler's Plantation near Woodhall is all that remains – and his 1,200 foot mineshaft in Woodhall never yielded any coal, and was allowed to fill with water.

But while Parkinson disappeared into obscurity, a local squire, Thomas Hotchkin, perhaps inspired by stories that ailing cattle drinking water from the mineshaft became well again, decided to harness these beneficial mineral waters. Thus Woodhall obtained its 'Spa', and its growth was spectacular. A Pump Room and Bath House were followed by two large hotels. In 1855 the railways brought even more people, and Woodhall Spa was wholly redesigned as a 'garden city'.

Today the spa has run dry – the well collapsed in 1983. The railways have deserted, and the Victoria and Royal hotels have been replaced by the Petwood and the Golf – and it is to golf that Woodhall looks to maintain its prosperity these days, the English Golfing Union now having their headquarters here.

2. Passing to the right of the spa buildings, you will see the Tea House in the Woods with its distinctive Mediterranean look. Immediately to its right a short path leads you to a clearer footpath, along which you turn left. Follow the squirrels! Sadly only grey these days. Fences each side guide you through the woods, and, as you pass behind the spa, you can make out something of its faded splendour. The way becomes lighter as the beautifully kept golf course appears on your right. Exercise your retina and try to spot the tall stone monument to the Duke of Wellington in the distance.

The Wellington Monument, a tall obelisk surmounted by a bust of the Iron Duke, was erected by a Colonel Richard Elmhirst in 1844, 29 years after the Waterloo triumph. The wood of oak trees behind the column is explained in the inscription, now virtually illegible:

'Waterloo Wood, raised from acorns sown immediately after the memorable Battle of Waterloo, where victory was achieved by that great captain of the age, His Grace the Duke of Wellington, commanding the British forces against the French arms commanded by Napoleon

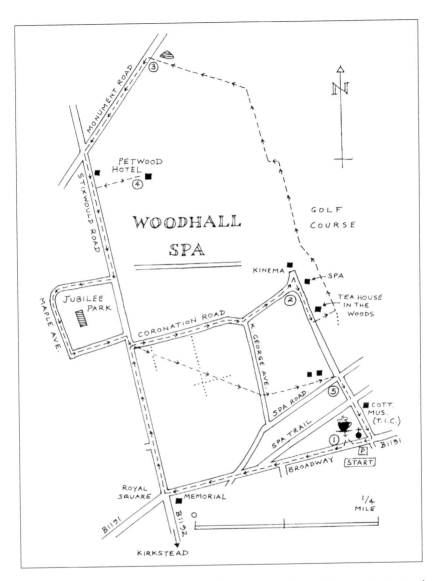

Bonaparte. The 18th of June 1815 which momentous victory gave general peace to Europe. This monument erected by Rd. E. 1844'

3. Just past a large pond on your right, dark and thick enough to be treacle, this charming path meets Monument Road, which is an avenue lined with enormous oak trees, and you turn left to follow it. The roadside is unpaved but wide and safe. High brick walls loom on the left and you become aware of the proximity of Petwood House. Follow these walls left at the crossroads, pass a secret gate and a half-timbered lodge, and arrive at the entrance drive to Petwood.

The origin of Petwood House's name could not be more trite, the country mansion having been built in 1905 by Grace Maple – later Lady Weigall – in her 'pet wood'. The appearance of this hotel, however, is breathtaking, a vast display of extravagant half-timbering outside, a showcase of oak panelling and wood carving inside. The gardens too are spectacular, with lawns, rhododendron walks and a lake leading to the woodland beyond. The war saw Petwood requisitioned by the Royal Air Force. The Squadron Bar is dedicated to the men of 617 Squadron and is full of memorabilia.

4. Leave Petwood and continue along Stixwould Road, then cross over to enter Maple Avenue.

Maple Avenue, named after Grace Maple, winds through Jubilee Park, which was donated to the town by the Weigalls in 1947 and is seemingly unchanged since. Featuring a heated open-air pool surrounded by pergolas and attractive gardens, the grounds also contain facilities for bowling, tennis, putting and cricket. More recently a caravan park and an area for gymkhanas and agricultural shows have been added.

Maple Avenue leads you back onto Stixwould Road and you will recognise Coronation Road once again leading into the woods opposite. Enter Coronation Road but instead of duplicating your route to the spa, accept the 'You are Welcome to Walk in the Woods' invitation and head diagonally into the trees on your right. Just pick a way through. If you keep anything like a true course you should cross a bridge, then King George Avenue, to emerge at the Spa Road and Coronation Road junction near a hall and tennis courts. Got lost? No matter – you'll find your way.

5. From here a brightly painted white gate takes you along a short path, at the end of which a further white gate belonging to the old railway takes you past the Cottage Museum and back to the Broadway. Look to your right here and you discover you have returned to within a few yards of the former garage, where you may receive your 'Just Desserts'.

Walk 13
STOCKWITH MILL

Alfred, Lord Tennyson was one of England's finest poets, becoming Poet Laureate in 1850, and seemingly every town and village in Lincolnshire claims a connection. But here is the walk that really does explore the countryside in which Tennyson was born, grew up and wrote some of his best loved works. Your journey through 'Tennyson Country' is long and varied, and leads you into the finest scenery the Lincolnshire Wolds has to offer. A series of attractive historic villages are linked by country paths which vary from broad rural byways to narrow muddy tracks – so adequate footwear is a must. You can expect to repeatedly ascend wind-blown crests only to plunge to another secluded tree-lined valley. At the end of this expedition what better way to relax than sitting outside a picturesque watermill teashop?

☕ Ideally, a fine day should be chosen for a visit to this teashop, because Stockwith Mill is best appreciated from the yard in front of the mill, overlooking the foaming mill-race shaded by tall swaying trees, as you try to distinguish the songs of the birds above the thundering noise of the water. What a wonderful place in which to enjoy a cream tea or a tempting slice of cake selected from the display inside. A full range of hot and cold meals is also available, and many include a buffet-style salad. If the elements drive you indoors, one of the excellent hot puddings will soon warm you, and on Sundays a full roast lunch can be ordered. Both rooms are given a farmhouse flavour by the red and black checked quarry tiles, and one has a welcoming open fire on cold days. Around the yard are shops selling crafts, gifts and plants. Opening times are as follows: March to October from 10.30 am to 6 pm on Tuesdays to Sundays (plus Bank Holiday Mondays); November until late December from 10.30 am to 5 pm on Thursdays to Sundays. Telephone: 01507 588221. When Stockwith Mill is not open, refreshment can be found at inns in Tetford, Raithby and Hagworthingham.

DISTANCE: 7 miles.

MAPS: OS Landranger 122 (Skegness) or Explorer 273 (Lincolnshire Wolds South).

STARTING POINT: Stockwith Mill, Hagworthingham (GR 358705).

HOW TO GET THERE: Hagworthingham is 6 miles east of Horncastle on the A158 to Skegness and, just east of the village, a side road leads you towards Harrington. Stockwith Mill is only one mile down this lane – the car park on the left is the first sighting of it. You may park here, but remember that when the teashop closes, so does the car park!

ALTERNATIVES: Park at Hagworthingham (point 2), Somersby (point 6) or Bag Enderby (point 7) to place the teashop partway round your walk – your parking is then not governed by any curfew. To lessen the distance, the OS maps shows obvious ways to short-cut past Somersby or Hagworthingham.

THE WALK

The watermill at Stockwith is set in its own valley, hidden by tall alders and reached by a bridge over the River Lymm. The mill dates from the 16th century, but sadly the waterflow is no longer sufficient to enable flour to be produced. A study of the gigantic undershot mill wheel will lead you behind the building to a series of trout ponds linked by a pleasant walk.

1. This adventure begins by turning right onto the road outside the mill, which in ½ mile reaches a footpath on the right. Follow this path to a clear sign at the track in front of you, where you cross another stile. Pass a peculiar gabled livestock hut, cross another stile and follow an improving path into Hagworthingham. Reaching an inn, the George and

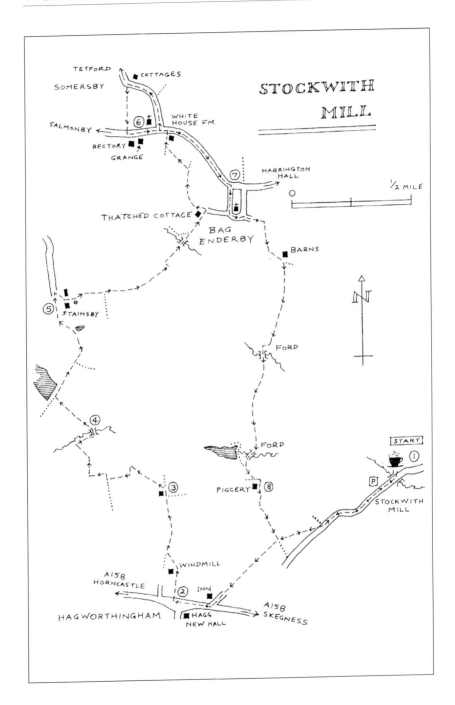

Dragon, walk to your right through the village, which is a Lincolnshire oddity in its lacking a dominant church tower or spire.

2. Opposite the imposing Hagg New Hall a short flight of steps leads you along a narrow shaded path and into an open field. Rounding the derelict ivy-coloured windmill and its sad outbuildings the footpath heads down to a lane, which you follow as far as a large cream house on the left. Now a wonderful view is unveiled across the valley before you, to Harrington Hall in the distance.

This large mellow red-brick hall was built in 1673 by the Amcotts, and restored recently following a huge blaze in 1991. Tennyson was a good friend of the Amcotts and a regular visitor. Harrington's walled terrace garden is thought to be the inspiration behind his poem 'Come into the garden, Maud', while Maud herself is believed to be Rosa Baring, the stepdaughter of the tenant of the Hall.

3. Past the stables to the right of the cream house your path heads diagonally across a thistly field and over a stile by a small steep combe. Follow the path left around the field edge to a lane and turn right onto this. Turn left to skirt another cornfield, and descend the steep hillside to the stream at the foot of the valley. This is a magical spot, and you follow the winding stream to the right, tall alders towering overhead, to cross the stream via a wooden footbridge.

4. Ascend the hill on a good path, with the hedge to your right and the church at Ashby Puerorum in view straight ahead. Soon you reach a chalky lane along which you turn right, passing a small man-made lake – here you may see swans, and even otters have been spotted by locals, allegedly. The chalk track wends its way up the hill between open fields, and just past a charming copse of trees on your right, you find yourself in the neat grounds of the farm at Stainsby.

5. The lane doubles back past the pony field and between the handsome brick farm buildings to continue down the hill. Passing a pond, you may become aware that you are being watched by scarecrows in the fields around you. However, unlike Faldingworth, these are real live working scarecrows, and you should not stare, but fix your gaze on the wood straight in front of you. Through this wood another field takes you to the River Lymm (one of several claiming to be Tennyson's 'Brook'). Cross via a small bridge and ascend a chalk track to a white thatched cottage.

Carefully locate the footpath between the barns to the left of this cottage and, after following a short curved field edge path, you will see your way branching left over the fields. Four stiles later this path brings you into a woodyard behind a large white house. Out of the yard and onto the road, turn left to enter Somersby.

The Tennyson story begins at Somersby, with his birth at the Rectory in 1809, and you will wish to stand at the gates of this rambling house and consider its importance. Far more striking architecturally, however, is its neighbour, Somersby Grange. Built of red brick in 1722 it has been attributed to Sir John Vanbrugh, famous for Blenheim Palace and Castle Howard – how much more fitting a birthplace for the Poet Laureate the towers and castellations of the Grange would have made. The small church perched on top of the hill across the road holds a bronze bust of Tennyson.

6. In front of the church turn right, pass the farm, and continue to two estate cottages on the right. Opposite these, a straight field path, affording good views of the three major buildings, takes you back to a road. Head left here through the heart of Somersby and along a leafy lane to Bag Enderby, a village heralded by an ancient tree-stump supposedly resembling a bear, but which could, from various angles, be interpreted as almost any animal.

7. Bag Enderby is a step back in time, silent and romantic, littered with wooden farm buildings and abandoned machinery amongst the trees. Two short parallel lanes run past cottages to the church and a range of interesting buildings opposite. A lane leads eastwards from the church, then descends through enormous trees at Barn Holt – a pair of barns built of the brightest orange bricks and roof tiles. Now follow this lane unerringly for the next mile or so, a roller-coaster ride alternately rising to show you the whole of the valley you have circled, then dipping to cross bridges at two fords so similar that the second induces a clear sense of deja-vu!

8. Rounding a hay-barn next to a piggery you soon realise that you are on the track you crossed on the outward journey. Retrace your route back to the bubbling mill streams of Stockwith and collapse into the teashop, where you will be rewarded for your strenuous efforts.

Walk 14
SPILSBY

Lincolnshire is surprisingly rich in history, and nowhere is more colourful in its heritage than Old Bolingbroke, the destination of this walk. Here is the birthplace of a king and the scene of many a bloody conflict, nowadays a serene village with a mere low ruin and a tale to tell. The pleasant market town of Spilsby has an equally fascinating – if less medieval – history and, of course, a fine small teashop. From here Bolingbroke is an exhilarating trek across the Wolds, and you will need to be suitably shod. The return journey is a more varied adventure, with typical Lincolnshire villages adding to the enjoyment of the Wolds countryside. The views are breathtaking from start to finish, while the sound of pealing church bells often fills the vast ever-changing skies overlooking the whole scene.

☕ To find Shaw's Tearoom you would not expect to look for a shop selling medals and silver cups. But if you walk through Centrepiece Trophies and Engraving you will find this excellent little teashop, clean and friendly, the perfect shelter from the bustle of the Market Place. Everything here is home-made, and the menu is varied and imaginative, ranging from Summer Spice – warm gingerbread with orange slices, stem ginger syrup and ice-cream – to the slightly less exotic Marmite Soldiers. A Specials board also lists the day's 'Wicked Treats', and the soup of the day (winter only). A good selection of fine teas and coffees, together with real china and fresh flowers on each table, complete the ambience. Shaw's is open between 9.30 am and 4 pm, except Tuesdays (10 am to 2 pm) and Sundays (closed). Telephone: 01507 588479, or the trophy shop can put you in touch with the tearoom (01790 753807).

When the tearoom is closed, alternative refreshment can be found in the inns around Spilsby's Market Place or the Black Horse in Old Bolingbroke.

DISTANCE: 8 miles.
MAPS: OS Landranger 122 (Skegness) or Explorer 273 (Lincolnshire Wolds South).
STARTING POINT: Shaw's Tearoom in Spilsby Market Place (GR 403662).
HOW TO GET THERE: Spilsby lies just off the A16, about 1½ miles south of the junction with the A158. Follow the signs into the Market Place. Centrepiece Trophies and Shaw's Tearoom are found towards the far end of the left-hand row of buildings. There is some parking in and around the Market Place plus a car park just behind.
ALTERNATIVES: Begin at the castle in Old Bolingbroke (picking up the route at point 5) – thus Spilsby becomes a welcome oasis halfway round the walk.

THE WALK

1. Walk back through the cheerful Market Place, nodding to the bronze statue of Sir John Franklin, then inspecting St James' church on the left and the old Grammar School on the right.

Sir John Franklin, Spilsby's most famous son, was born in 1786 in a house overlooking the Market Place. Having joined the Royal Navy at the age of 14 he enjoyed an illustrious naval career, which included service at the Battle of Trafalgar. He was knighted for his services at 42, and set sail in 1845 to locate the North-West Passage, but both of his ships became entrapped by the Arctic ice, and Franklin perished, along with his entire crews. Many years later missions were sent to discover what had befallen the expedition, and from their findings it has become accepted that Franklin did in fact find the Passage. As well as his statue, a plaque on the bakery wall denotes his birthplace, and a monument to him can be found in the church. The church also contains important tombs and memorials

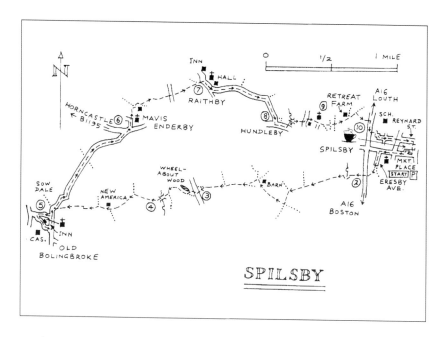

SPILSBY

to the Willoughby family, who lived at nearby Eresby Hall until it was destroyed by fire in 1769.

Next on your right is a most extraordinary sight, the four massive Doric columns of the Greek-style portico of the former Sessions House, now a thriving theatre. Turning left opposite a hotel into Eresby Avenue, follow the course of the once grand approach to Eresby Hall (now breached by the bypass) almost as far as the sports ground. Here, head under a large sycamore on your right to emerge from the trees by the side of the main road. Cross carefully and remain alert to locate a white post on the roadside.

2. Stride into the fields in front of you, detouring around an unbridged ditch along the way. At a marked post the route, now clearer, heads to a fork, opts left, continues to a crossroads and turns right. Here, in summer, an unexpected plantation of sunflowers, along with a chalky track winding into the distance and views to high trees on the horizon, gives the walk a brief flavour of Tuscany. But a little further along, turning left just past a grey barn, you are undeniably back on a Lincolnshire lane. Follow this track to a road – the footpath cuts the last corner through the field on the left.

3. Over the road continue on a path, rather casual at first, keeping a lake set in a landscaped arboretum to your right (Wheelabout Wood). Soon, a footpath to the right leaves the curving track and careers down the hillside to cross a stream and ascend an idyllic meadow on the other side.

4. Now follow the trail to another fork, turn left and pursue a rather vague path through a field, bringing you to a more obvious fenced path, which winds along below a wooded bank. At a gate past the deserted farm at New America the track becomes a path once more, and descends towards Old Bolingbroke. On your left the intimate views over sheep pastures sloping down to the wooded riverside below give way to a vast panorama stretching to the distant Stump at Boston. You reach the road near to Sow Dales Nature Reserve. Turn left to stroll into Old Bolingbroke and bear right to pass the church. Now a lane to the left leads you past the Black Horse Inn to the evocative ruins of the castle.

Old Bolingbroke was a thriving market town in medieval times and its castle has the honour of being the only place in Lincolnshire to witness the birth of a king. Henry IV was born here in 1366, the son of John of Gaunt and his cousin Blanche, heiress to the Earl of Lancaster – also Lord of Bolingbroke. But by the 15th century the castle was falling into decline and it was largely dismantled after the Civil War, when Royalist forces at Bolingbroke capitulated following Cromwell's victory at nearby Winceby. Now the ruined castle is a haunting tribute to its war-torn history. Still impressive, the five towers, the gatehouse and the moat serve as a reminder that this is one of Lincolnshire's most important relics.

5. Leave the village by the same road along which you entered, this time continuing up Spilsby Hill until you reach the main road 1½ miles later. Directly opposite you a tiny lane leads down into Mavis Enderby.

6. Passing St Michael's church to the right, with its sundial and restored medieval cross, look for a 'secret' stile in a leafy corner on the left. Here a white iron rail guides you around a large secluded house to a range of tumbledown wooden stables behind. Passing to the left and round the back of the stables, seek a hidden path branching left to a stile in the hedgerow – if you reach a locked gate you've missed it! Over the stile keep the hedge on your right as you walk between the trees down to a stream then up to a fence. Now into a totally different landscape of cultivated soil, you cross a series of fields and one road before joining a lane heading into Raithby.

Impressive buildings abound in the tiny village of Raithby. As well as a fine traditional inn and the church of the Holy Trinity – enlarged and restructured in 1873 – you will find the stately Raithby Hall. This was built for the Brackenburys in 1776 and features a modest but treasured Methodist chapel, created by John Wesley in 1779. The stable block housing the chapel can be clearly viewed from the roadside, as can the front of the Hall – through a stunning gateway. The Hall is not open to the public, however, and entry is on the grounds of infirmity as it is now a nursing home.

7. Turn right through this well-wooded village. Opposite Laundry Lane the advertised footpath does not exist and you should continue with care all the way along the lane to Hundleby.

8. Here turn left onto the main road as far as a footpath next to a tree-lined stream on the left. This short riverside stretch emerges to run alongside the nearby gardens to a village road, where opposite you and slightly to your left is Spindleberry Cottage. A narrow hedged path to the left of the cottage leads you past the ironstone church of St Mary with iron gates guarding its approach on the other side of your path.

9. Continuing on the same path, two stiles now lead you past a farm and over a new road to bring you onto another farm track on its way to Retreat Farm. Shortly beyond this farm a narrow path departs from the track to the right, and soon regains the main A16 road. Turn right onto this and pass the large school playing field.

10. At a rusty iron gate just past the school a shady path leads you into a residential area, now close to the centre of Spilsby. Woodlands Avenue is easy to locate and it continues as a passage to a main road. Now walk down Reynard Street until you spot a narrow alley by the side of a supermarket, which brings you back into the Market Place. Your achievement should be recognised by a substantial treat at the teashop, and maybe a small trophy from the shop next door.

Walk 15
LOUTH

Seen from miles around, the Wolds' finest spire heralds the presence of historic Louth, the 'Capital of the Wolds', situated where the River Lud flows down from the hills to the wide coastal plain below. It is a fascinating town built of red brick and pantiles, with a thriving Market Place and splendid Georgian and Victorian architecture. This walk starts outside Louth and visits the teashop midway, reached via a dramatic wooded gorge with a poignant story to tell. The outward leg is a high-level switchback with the return being a gentle riverside stroll, and in the middle of it all is a trip back in time in the most wonderful traditional teashop.

Chuzzlewits may call its sandwiches 'continental style', but make no mistake, this is the most quintessentially English of teashops. The glass-front of this listed building housed a restaurant in the 1900s, and the name of the original owners – Forman's – can still be seen in the porch mosaic. Today it is a family affair, with waitresses in immaculate black and white uniforms transporting you back to Victorian times. The elegant atmosphere created by the period décor and chandeliers is enhanced by tall palms and plants, and each table has fresh flowers, white china and silver cutlery. The food is quality indeed – it is, of course, all freshly prepared here. Moreover everything is beautifully presented, and even a slice of gateau arrives with a fresh fruit garnish. The continental-style sandwiches contain truly exotic fillings, with cheeses prominent – Gruyère, Emmental and Parmesan are just some – while bacon and mushroom bagels are also very much in demand. There are versions of afternoon tea to suit every taste, and whichever tea or coffee you care to name – Chuzzlewits is a touch of class and a real treat. Opening times are 9.30 am to 5 pm from Tuesday to Saturday, all year round, and Sundays in summer. Telephone: 01507 611171. If by some misfortune you find Chuzzlewits closed, Louth's numerous restaurants will not disappoint you.

DISTANCE: 3 miles.

MAPS: OS Landranger 122 (Skegness) or Explorer 282 (Lincolnshire Wolds North).

STARTING POINT: The car park at the Hallington end of Hubbard's Hills (GR 316860).

HOW TO GET THERE: The town of Louth is 17 miles south of Grimsby on the A16 and is easily located – not least by its dominating spire. Depart from Louth town centre in the direction of Horncastle (A153) and turn right after a mile at an octagonal white toll-house. The car park is on your right 400 yards down this lane.

ALTERNATIVES: The walk could be extended south from the car park – maybe as far as Raithby. To begin the walk at the teashop you should seek one of the many public car parks around the centre of Louth and pick up the route at point 3.

THE WALK

1. From the car park, go through the gate to enter Hubbard's Hills. Immediately look to your right and climb the flight of steps you see ascending the steep bank. Cut left near the top of these to join a wonderful bank-top path, carpeted with bark chippings. From this path the views are stunning, especially in autumn. Beyond the golf course to your right the spire stands majestic, but through the tall trees to your left the sight of the river below and the woods on the far bank is breathtaking.

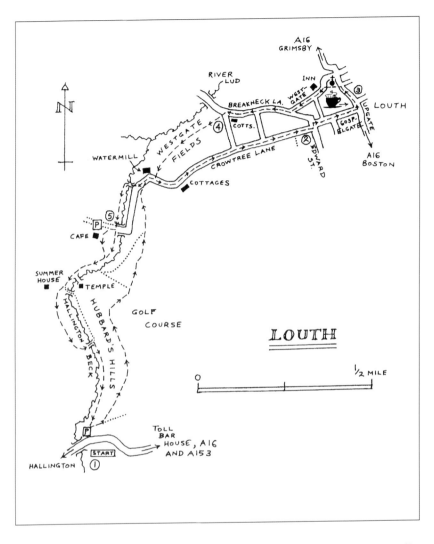

Two hundred and fifty years might sound like a long time, but that is all it took for the 125 foot deep valley of Hubbard's Hills to form at the end of the last Ice Age. This spectacular gorge was created 40,000 years ago as torrents of glacial meltwater cut through the chalk. The volume of water was such that the steep-sided valley was shaped in a comparatively short period of time.

Enjoying this bird's-eye view of the sights you will meet on your return through the valley, you eventually descend to a road, guided by a dunnnage fence. In front of you is the attractive Old Mill House, recently restored, and you bear right to follow Crowtree Lane until it terminates at Edward Street.

2. A prompt left-right at Edward Street takes you into Gospelgate – named, curiously, after the nearby 'goose pool', and not from any ecclesiastical connection. At the end of Gospelgate you will find yourself in Upgate. Can you smell the cakes? Can you hear the kettle? – Chuzzlewits is just a few yards to your left.

3. Outside the door of Chuzzlewits follow Upgate left to the large wrought iron gates leading into the cobbled close of St James' church. In front of you is a most spectacular and unforgettable sight, with the hexagonal spire soaring almost 300 feet into the Lincolnshire sky.

Accolades by Pevsner as 'one of the most majestic of English parish churches' and by Betjeman as 'one of the last great medieval Gothic masterpieces' are matched by the church's own claim to be the tallest parish church in the country. Built of Ancaster stone in 1634 its height of 295 feet was not achieved until 1844, when the spire was renewed following a lightning strike – the old spire now rests, appropriately, in the vicarage garden. Views of the gracefully buttressed spire are particularly memorable when it is illuminated by floodlighting. Among the carved stone heads on the south face, look for Canon Aidan Ward, who was Rector in 1960. You will know when you have found him – he's wearing spectacles!

Opposite Canon Ward is a plaque commemorating the Louth Uprising of 1536. This was part of Lincolnshire's reaction to Henry VIII's Dissolution of the Monasteries – which embraced the abbey at Louth. But the rebellion was swiftly quashed and resulted in many executions, including that of the Vicar of Louth, Thomas Kendall, at Tyburn.

The road ahead of you is Westgate, and every building is a delight worth inspecting – the Rectory on the left and the Wheatsheaf on the right, built in 1625, deserve particular attention. Westgate runs into Breakneck Lane and past further interesting buildings to a row of neat brick cottages on the left just before the River Lud.

4. Now go through a gate in the white picket fence opposite to enter Westgate Fields. This riverside meadow, with mown lawns and specimen trees all around, leads you back to the Old Mill House, where you climb to exit the field onto Crowtree Lane once more. Now walk past the mill and cross a bridge leading onto a good footpath with Hallington Beck running alongside. About 200 yards down this path you re-enter Hubbard's Hills.

5. Choose between the higher path, where you will find a charming wooden refreshment hut, completely untouched by progress since the 1950s (and still serving home-made ice-lollies!), and the riverside path – here noisy mallard will insist upon a toll-fee of bread crusts before you may pass. Both paths meet at a fence where gigantic trees part to reveal the valley proper before you. Continue alongside the river, spanned by stepping-stones and a series of narrow bridges. In summer expect to negotiate groups of children running between the water and their picnic blankets – a scene unchanged for generations. Look out for a drinking fountain in the form of a Classical temple, and 'gingerbread' summer-houses on both banks.

Hard to believe that these cheerful surroundings have grown from a legacy of tragedy. A Swiss teacher travelling through Europe was halted at Louth when he fell in love with a local farmer's daughter. Auguste Pahud and Annie Grant were married in 1877 and lived in bliss until Annie died suddenly during a trip to London 12 years later. Auguste was a broken man and lived as a recluse for the next 13 years, before hanging himself with the cord of his own dressing-gown. His will decreed that part of his considerable estate should go towards the purchase of Hubbard's Hills as a lasting gift to the people of Louth, with a series of provisos that meant the area would always remain unspoilt. The fountain temple contains the commemorative stone laid by the people of Louth and unveiled at the extravagant opening celebration in 1907.

Just before the path crosses the stream, head up the grass bank on your right and round the back of a small wood. At the end of the wood you descend to another bridge, cross the stream, then follow the shaded path until you find yourself back at the car park, and your journey's end.

Walk 16
TEALBY

Tealby, with its wealth of mellow stone buildings, is accepted to be one of Lincolnshire's most attractive villages. The River Rase, which rises high above, cascades through it via a series of mills, fords and waterfalls. Our walk, however, leaves the valley behind and follows the contours of the Wolds foothills to the twin churches of nearby Walesby. Admire the splendid views towards the cathedral at Lincoln, which disappears gradually from sight as you descend into the village, and tea at the Tealby Tearooms.

 Front Street is an appealing collection of traditional stone and brick cottages, in the centre of which stand the Tealby Tearooms, brightly painted and impossible to miss. All the baking is done by the proprietor, and he will tell you that not only does he pick the mushrooms for his mushroom soup but that he also 'gathers' the ingredients for his renowned game soup! His cakes and plum loaf are equally tasty and a range of sandwiches and light meals are available. The tearooms are open every Sunday and bank holiday from 10.30 am to 5.30 pm. From

April to September they are also open on Saturdays (from 10.30 am) and weekdays (from 2.30 pm) – closed on ordinary Mondays. Telephone: 01673 838261. If the teashop is not open you will find two inns in the village. Both serve hot food.

DISTANCE: 5 miles.
MAPS: OS Landranger 113 (Grimsby) or Explorer 282 (Lincolnshire Wolds North).
STARTING POINT: Free car park at the Tennyson D'Eyncourt Village Hall in Tealby (GR 158908).
HOW TO GET THERE: Tealby is just north-east of Market Rasen on the Grimsby road, the B1203. Turn off south at the church and a few yards down the hill the village hall and car park are visible on your left.
ALTERNATIVES: Park by the roadside in Walesby and begin the walk there. Your teashop visit will then be in the middle of the walk. From Tealby the walk could be halved by ascending directly to Risby at point 3 and continuing from point 7.

THE WALK
The Tennyson D'Eyncourt Village Hall is a legacy of a noble local family. But their most extraordinary contribution to the village came from the fanciful imagination of Charles Tennyson D'Eyncourt, an uncle of the Poet Laureate Alfred, Lord Tennyson. Upon inheriting the estate of Bayons Manor in 1835 he converted his modest home into an enormous romantic folly – a Gothic castle, complete with drawbridge, portcullis and moat. The army, who had requisitioned the manor in the Second World War, paid one last visit in 1965 – this time to blow up what was left of the decaying ruin. Today a few perimeter walls stand amidst the dense trees, but sadly no trace of the manor itself can be found.

1. Leaving the car park, turn right up the hill then left onto the road to Market Rasen. Just past White Cottage on your right a track leads you to a gate and diagonally across a meadow. After crossing a stile you now leave the Viking Way to cross a bridge on your left and climb to the next stile.

Follow a narrow path through the next two fields.

2. Crossing the chalk track leading up to Castle Farm keep to the fence until the footpath veers into the field and heads for a gap in the hedge ahead – follow the cane poles here! A bridge and stile bring you back onto grass. Continue across these meadows to the tarmac track and turn left to join Catskin Lane.

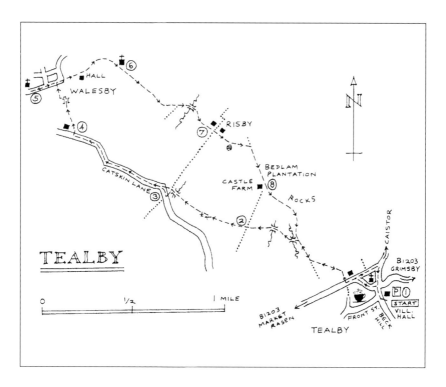

3. Turn right onto this lane and in about ⅓ mile cross a stile on your right, which leads you to a grassy field path.

4. As you begin to descend to another stile and bridge you will espy All Saints' Church, more commonly known as the Ramblers' Church, looming high to your right. But your path leads you around a fenced paddock and along a short wooded stretch to emerge through a gap in the stone wall into the heart of Walesby. A few yards to your left is this tiny village's second delightful church, that of St Mary and All Saints.

Walesby's two churches are in sharp contrast to each other. The 12th century Ramblers' Church lost its 'parish church' title in 1914. Though restored in 1930, the medieval atmosphere here is still powerful during the occasional candlelit services, especially the magical Christmas Carol festivals. The rambling connection is provided by a stained glass window depicting walkers and cyclists. Down in the village the new parish church of St Mary and All Saints, built in 1913 in the Arts and Crafts tradition, is remarkable for its row of large central pillars. Notice the heart motifs cut

77

from the wooden shutters of the tower windows.

5. Having visited the newer church, retrace your steps, pass the gap in the wall and, where the road turns left, continue dead straight ahead. This leafy track is surfaced at first, but once past Walesby Hall a muddy trail takes over as you are led up the hill and out of the trees. Passing 'Pignut Field' on your left, you now become aware that the Ramblers' Church is watching your every step once again. When you reach the foot of its squat tower, it is worth an exploration at close quarters.

6. Exit the churchyard by the far gate, climb up the hill to one stile and cross an arable field to reach another at the end of the woods of ash and sycamore. The footpath here heads obliquely down an attractive grassy bank through trees and bushes. Yellow waymarkers will assist you until you reach the foot of the hill. Now the way is clear. You walk through a gap in the high bushes, then over a stile, a bridge, another stile, and climb steeply up the opposite side of the valley. The path levels and heads towards the hamlet of Risby.

7. Explore the courtyard with the Hall on your left and the farm buildings on your right before rejoining the Viking Way at the cattle grid and turning left. Hug the fence to avoid the marsh, pass through a gate near a small pond and head upwards to the corner of the field. Should you have forgotten the purpose of your mission, a white wooden board proclaiming the delights of the Tealby Tearooms here affirms your resolve. With renewed energy you now hurdle a series of four stiles to emerge at a farm.

Castle Farm, despite its battlements and Gothic windows, was constructed in the early 19th century as an eyecatcher for the occupants of Bayons Manor. The farm cuts a striking silhouette from whichever angle it is viewed, but too close an inspection should be avoided – the owners are very sensitive to intruders.

8. Turning left at the farm, choose between the valley and a higher path guarded by two impressive Scots pines. Both routes bring you to the same gate into the next field, passing rocky outcrops on your left. Soon you will recognise the bridge to your right and you retrace your steps to the main road. This time, stray around the back of the church of All Saints before regaining the crossroads, or, better still, climb the steps to enter the churchyard where the path takes you directly to the same junction. From your journey across a land of Vikings and castles, return to Front Street and your well-earned cream tea at the Tearooms!

Walk 17
MARKET RASEN

Market Rasen is an unpretentious town with several excellent inns and the splendid Jossals Coffee Shop, reached halfway round this walk. Enchanting paths through two dense woodland areas are the highlight of the route, but a variety of more open scenery is encountered too, giving the walker wonderful views to the trees and church towers high on the Lincolnshire Wolds. This easy-to-follow circuit is fairly level and barred by not one stile!

Queen Street curves gently towards the Market Place in a succession of interesting old shop fronts and vernacular buildings, one of them the attractive low frontage of Jossals Coffee Shop and Bistro. Inside, pine tables and walls of terracotta give a Mediterranean feel. Everything in a comprehensive selection of hot and cold meals is freshly prepared to order, from the baguette stuffed with chicken tikka to the full Sunday lunch. A blackboard announces which soup, cakes and pies are available each day, plus other special dishes. Jossals is open from 9 am to 4 pm on Monday to Saturday and noon to 2 pm on Sundays – it is also open as a Bistro on Friday and Saturday evenings. Telephone: 01673 844221.

If Jossals is closed Market Rasen contains several alternative inns and restaurants.

DISTANCE: 5½ miles.
MAPS: OS Landranger 113 (Grimsby) or Explorer 282 (Lincolnshire Wolds North).
STARTING POINT: The Willingham Woods car park on the B1203 (GR 128902).
HOW TO GET THERE: Market Rasen is situated just off the A46 midway between Grimsby and Lincoln. Through the town turn left at the traffic lights, follow the B1203 for 1½ miles, and locate a small car park on the right at the side of the woods just past Poplars Farm.
ALTERNATIVES: Jossals could feature at the beginning or the end of your expedition, in which case you would park in Rasen's Market Place or one of several town centre car parks and pick up the route in point 3. Further exploration of Willingham Woods is recommended if time allows.

THE WALK

1. From the small car park walk left along the road towards Market Rasen, then bear right onto a lane just before Poplars Farm, noting that there are no poplars to be seen! Continue along this track into the woods, straight over a road and past a secluded caravan site. Continue ahead through more woods to a brick railway bridge (Nova Scotia Bridge), surprisingly grand, then about-turn to follow a lesser path in the same direction as the railway.

2. Often muddy, this path leads you through an enchanting tangled forest before turning sharp right to a level-crossing. Carefully over the tracks the path soon bends left to return towards the railway and the two meet at a second crossing. Safely over this your path, now tree-lined, curves right and progresses to a road.

3. Follow this road directly into Market Rasen. Turn right at the traffic lights into Queen Street and beyond the railway bridge you come to Jossals on the left, with a warm welcome awaiting you inside.

'The sleepiest town in England' was the impression made on Charles Dickens by Market Rasen. Now more commonly associated with National Hunt racing, Rasen has been a market town since 1215, before which it was known as East Rasen. It takes its name from the River Rase which flows from the Wolds towards the three Rasens – Market, Middle and West.

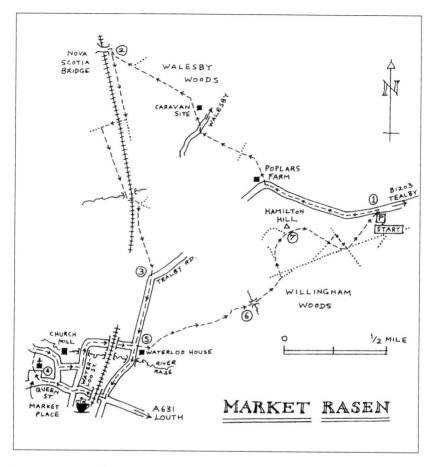

Now continue along Queen Street as far as the Market Place, passing a variety of interesting shop façades on the way. Behind the market shed at the rear of the square a passageway takes you past the ironstone church of St Thomas.

4. The River Rase runs behind the church past a handsome range of brick mill buildings, now restored to their former glory.

The four-storeyed Church Mill was originally built in 1830 as a warehouse, not a mill. An ambitious plan was hatched to link the River Ancholme with Market Rasen by a canal but was doomed to failure by the arrival of the railway in 1846. In truth, the building's alternative career

81

as a mill was no more successful, and a catalogue of problems led to its closure in 1959. It has since undergone a thorough restoration programme, and remains a handsome piece of Victorian industrial architecture.

To the right of the mill buildings Church Street leads you into Waterloo Street, which you follow to the left, over the Rase once more, soon finding yourself back on the main road.

5. On the opposite side of the main road enter the driveway to Waterloo House then look for a narrow footpath continuing along its left-hand edge. At the time of writing this section is undergoing development by the water authorities, but the footpath remains in place and brings you onto a path along the edge of arable fields. The route across the last field is indistinct, but the entrance into the woods opposite is easily located.

6. Here a sandy path leads you through gorse and oak, bearing left past yellow-marked posts, and ascending a winding track through the deciduous wood to the tower at the top of Hamilton Hill. Here a short detour to the left offers you a splendid view over the woods at Walesby and the Wolds beyond.

Hamilton Hill is said to be the place where two rebel forces from Louth and Caistor met and camped for the night in October 1536, during the futile Lincolnshire Rising against Henry VIII's Dissolution activities. Driven by fears of what hardships his policies might bring they were marching towards Lincoln. Their rebellion, however, was short-lived, and won them only a royal slur, the dismissal of Lincolnshire folk as 'the most brutal and beastly of our realm'.

7. Back at the tower head down the hillside, still following the yellow waymarkers, until you arrive at a meeting of several paths near the foot of the hill. From this junction the narrow permissive path to your left, shaded by tall trees, guides you straight back to the car park.

Willingham Woods and Walesby Woods occupy much of the land to the north and east of Rasen. Wildlife flourishes here – kestrels and other birds of prey can be seen around the wood's edges, and owls, jays and woodpeckers are also present. You may spot squirrels, stoats, weasels and hedgehogs – if you're lucky maybe even a fallow deer.

Walk 18
KIRTON-IN-LINDSEY

Nikolaus Pevsner and the Ordnance Survey still declare Mount Pleasant Windmill as derelict. Nothing could be further from the truth. The traditional brick tower mill is now fully restored and there is no better way to watch its sails proudly turning than over fresh tea or coffee from the excellent teashop in the courtyard. Setting out along the slopes of the Lincoln Cliff you will enjoy splendid views over the Trent Valley below, to return on a lower route via woods and lanes.

It goes without saying that everything sold in the Mill Teashop is baked using the stoneground organic flour from Mount Pleasant Windmill itself. Through a wall of glass the teashop overlooks a terraced area, where you can enjoy your tea or coffee, accompanied by a slice of fruit loaf or a scone. The carrot cake is especially delicious and the sandwiches are mountainous. Under the same roof is an excellent wholefood shop, and next door is the bakery. The teashop, bakery and mill are open from 10 am to 5 pm on weekends and bank holidays and

11 am to 4 pm on Fridays, with extended hours during August. Telephone: 01652 640177.

When the teashop is closed, there are inns in Kirton offering refreshment, as well as the Sutton Arms in Scawby to the north-east and Briggate Lodge at the junction of the A15 and the A18.

DISTANCE: 7½ miles.
MAPS: OS Landranger 112 (Scunthorpe) or Explorer 280.
STARTING POINT: Mount Pleasant Windmill near Kirton-in-Lindsey (GR 939994).
HOW TO GET THERE: The B1398 runs from Scunthorpe to Lincoln parallel to the Roman Ermine Street (A15) and passes through Kirton-in-Lindsey 8 miles south of Scunthorpe. From Scunthorpe take the A18 past the Steelworks, and halfway up the hill turn onto the B1398 where Kirton is signposted. The Windmill cannot be missed on your right ½ mile before Kirton town.
ALTERNATIVES: Manton is a good alternative starting point (point 4). Kirton-in-Lindsey station is another and offers better parking.

THE WALK

The current Mount Pleasant Windmill was built on top of the round-house of the former postmill. Now a more typical Lincolnshire mill, its brick tower is covered with numerous layers of tar to prevent water from penetrating the brickwork. The quartet of original sails turned from 1875 to 1936, when they were replaced by a 20 hp oil engine – itself retired in 1973, when trading ceased. The decline in fortunes was arrested in 1987, when an ambitious restoration programme was begun. Thompson's of Alford were the millwrights given the task of constructing the new cap and sails, and in March 1991 the wind once again rotated them. The mill tower can be ascended for a fascinating insight into how the organic flour is made.

1. Turning right onto the road outside the mill yard you soon spot a stile into the field on your right. Head down the hillside looking for a barred gate in the hedge on your right. Beyond this you cross a large field to a stile on the right of a conspicuous red-roofed house. Through a horse paddock and across a lane via two more stiles, you descend the railway embankment diagonally.

2. Your path scrambles up the opposite bank, then leads you through bushes to bring you into an open paddock. Through the next gate the path follows a hedge on the left of a meadow, then into a large, wide field. Admiring the view of the splendid ivy-clad Mount Pleasant high on the hillside to your right, you come to a track where you will identify your

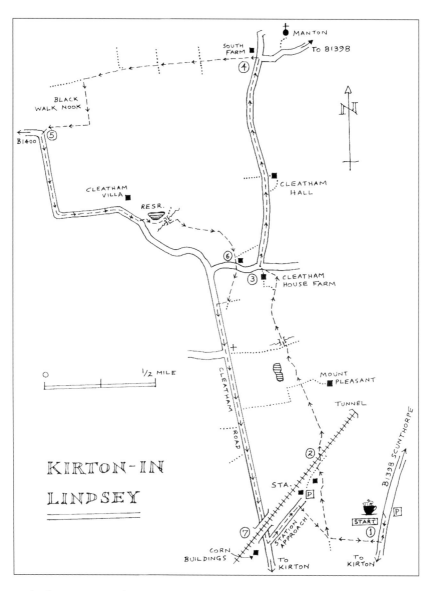

path diving into a thorny wood mid-way between two telegraph poles. The path becomes less restricted and passes a large fishing lake on the left before emerging from the undergrowth onto another track. Cross a railed plank-bridge into the next field and go straight ahead to join a road with Cleatham House Farm on your left.

3. Passing the farm on the road, look for a side-road signposted to Manton, which leads you to Cleatham Hall.

Of Cleatham Hall's grand pediments and pillars little can be seen, but the surrounding grounds will capture your imagination. On the roadside a manicured lawn area gives way to high railings and a walled moat-like channel. Broad stone gateposts bear a heavy white wooden gate, opening onto a curving driveway, and a variety of trees and shrubs includes amazing topiary.

Now a row of some fifteen colossal beech trees guides you towards the village of Manton where, unless you wish to explore the village and its church, you turn left onto a broad lane just before South Farm.

4. This lovely fern-lined lane leads you downhill for a mile, passing woods on the left and overlooking lakes on the right. Reaching a bridleway on the left you enter a wood – Black Walk Nook.

Following the arrow-posts through this wood, you turn right near to its edge, and eventually depart from the wood onto an open road.

5. Turn left and follow this road for over a mile, passing Cleatham Villa then taking a footpath on the left next to a clump of very tall trees. This path leads you round the base of a small unseen reservoir before crossing a bridge on the right into a large field. Follow the edge of this field left for ½ mile, with the hedge alongside you, to emerge through a gap in the bushes onto a road next to timbered cottages.

6. Opposite you the footpath continues across a field for a short distance and onto a track leading to the road on your right. Turn left onto this perfectly straight road and contnue until you pass underneath the railway bridge.

7. Examine the impressive range of brick corn buildings on the right, before turning sharp left into the station approach road. The station itself is a superbly proportioned brick building, now maintained as a private property. On the other side of the courtyard in front of it a gap in the hedge leads you back into a field that you will recognise from the early stages of the walk. Now climb the hill and retrace your steps back to the teashop.

Walk 19
ASHBY-CUM-FENBY

This big adventure of a walk has got the lot! Starting on the Lincolnshire coastal plain you climb into the hills of the Wolds proper to gain breathtaking views as far as the North Sea. You set out from Ashby-cum-Fenby with its modern teashop amidst old farm buildings. Four other charming villages, typical of the Wolds, mark out the four corners of the walk. Trees of all types are everywhere, especially in the parkland near Barnoldby-le-Beck. Among the jewels you will come across are a beautiful wooded valley, a delightful stream, a series of interesting village churches and the area's best little ice-cream shop!

It must be said that Hall Farm offers the perfect setting for a teashop. The approach promises much – a leafy lane, a quaint old church, Hall Farm itself as a backdrop and hidden behind, a gravelled courtyard surrounded by a range of renovated brick farm buildings. This is where you will find Roosters. The interior resembles a spacious old barn, with iron roof struts and prominent wooden beams and pillars. In contrast to these there are bright walls and contemporary fabrics, and the atmosphere is cheerful and comfortable. A good range of main meals is offered, and the roasted lamb shank is particularly tasty – and filling! If you're going for the lot why not try the mussels to start – an enormous bowl arrives with a choice of sauces. Sandwiches come on ciabatta, baguette or granary bread, while in summer, afternoon tea on the sunny terraced courtyard outside is the order of the day, with cakes and puddings swelling the usual selection of pastries and scones. Although open all day most days, you should telephone to confirm opening times: 01472 220666. If Roosters is closed try the Ship at Barnoldby-le-Beck or other inns in nearby Waltham or Holton-le-Clay.

DISTANCE: 7½ miles.
MAPS: OS Landranger 113 (Grimsby) or Explorer 282 (Lincolnshire Wolds North) and 284.
STARTING POINT: Roosters bistro at Hall Farm in Ashby-cum-Fenby (GR 254011).
HOW TO GET THERE: Just north-east of the A18 crossroads on the B1203 Market Rasen-Grimsby road, turn off where Ashby-cum-Fenby is signposted, at the bottom of Ashby Hill. 'Roosters' is clearly indicated on your left at the first bend, but you should continue and park in the village as the small car park becomes very full.
ALTERNATIVES: There is parking in all four of the other villages listed. Any of these might successfully be used as a base for the walk, with the teashop then partway round.

THE WALK
The quiet village of Ashby-cum-Fenby has many delightful corners, but you will discover the best along the shaded lane leading to Roosters. Facing each other on the right of the lane are the ancient stone church of St Peter, containing a particularly beautiful medieval oak screen, and the Wray Almshouses. As you pass Hall Farm, built in Georgian times, look for the distinctive arched Venetian windows.

1. From the village of Ashby-cum-Fenby walk back along the quiet lane towards the main Binbrook to Grimsby road for ¼ mile. Just past Hall Farm Cottages on your left a finger-post on the right inscribed 'Wanderlust Way' beckons you through a kissing-gate into a meadow.

Now make a bee-line for the far left-hand corner of the field and another kissing-gate beneath five tall poplar trees. You are now in Brigsley. Cross

Waithe Beck and the main road to reach a small shop on the left.

2. Delicious home-made ice-cream no doubt having delayed your progress, you follow a path round the side of this building and through a stable courtyard via two stiles. You are now confined to an extremely narrow path – furthermore this path slopes down alarmingly from right to left, and would be ideally suited to walkers with legs of unequal length! The path is, however, easy to follow and soon hugs the edge of more spacious pastures before developing into a lovely grassy band between open fields. At a 'T-junction' of these paths turn right up a hill, and in another 100 yards, left along a path with a hedge and clumps of trees to its right.

Eventually a plantation of new trees comes in from the left to meet

89

your path, which now improves to a clear track through long grass and bushes, with tall trees on both sides. The path is halted abruptly at a new wooden fence where you are guided to the right and around the perimeter of a large property. Two kissing-gates later you emerge between a tiny farm office and an impressive white manor house into Barnoldby-le-Beck.

Barnoldby-le-Beck was a fief of the Pelhams from Brocklesby Hall (10 miles distant along Barton Street) and Pelham House in the village was one of their hunting lodges. If you visit St Helen's church in Barnoldby to view its historic south doorway, dated 1200, you will see another Brocklesby link at the churchyard gate. A granite obelisk was erected by friends of the popular William Smith, Huntsman to the Earl of Yarborough. At this spot in 1845, though a fine master of horse and hounds, he was thrown from his steed and died four days later from the head wounds he received.

The village also has strong Quaker connections, with many local families amongst the Pilgrim Fathers who set sail for America to escape religious persecution – maybe here is a clue to the origin of the name of the village inn – the Ship. Prosperous nowadays, Barnoldby-le-Beck is earning a reputation as a playground for millionaires – and lottery winners!

3. Turn left onto the road and, beyond the bends, look for a footpath sign directing you along a driveway to the left. A bridge on your right then takes you to a fenced path around a garden, and over a stile into an open field. Follow the fence at first, then head across the meadow to another stile hidden behind two large trees. Now bear left along the good track towards Manor Farm, but instead of entering the grounds, your path takes a sharp right alongside a wooden fence. Continue along this fence for ⅓ mile with rolling parkland visible between the trees on your left. At the corner of the field the footpath plunges under a large sycamore and remains in wooded shade until it reaches Barton Street.

4. Cross the road to a delightful spot overlooking a row of renovated cottages, whose proudly tended gardens run down to the miniature waterfalls of Waithe Beck. The track continues beside the fast-flowing stream, which will accompany you for the next 1½ miles. Past the interesting cluster of mill buildings the path now winds along the ivy-carpeted riverbank beneath a variety of trees forming arches and tunnels above your head. On the opposite bank lush meadows rise to tall distant trees. When the shade gives way to airy open fields, the footpath follows a straightforward course only leaving the stream a few yards before the next road is reached. Here a gap in the hedge by a house takes you onto the road and into the attractive village of Hatcliffe, full of tiny bridges over the roadside stream.

5. Follow the road through Hatcliffe, past the church and on until, at a cattle-grid on your left, a narrow road heads into the deeply wooded Ravendale Valley. Along this enchanting lane admire the variety of ancient trees closing in on both banks. Passing through a natural amphitheatre you exit the gorge at another cattle-grid.

6. Now simply follow this lovely lane for a further mile as far as the crossroads at East Ravendale, passing en route Priory Farm on the right and a spectacular chalk quarry face on the left.

Behind the farm you can spot the remnants of the 13th century priory, which formed part of the dowry given to Henry IV by his queen, Joan of Navarre. All that remains is the romantic overgrown ruin of a small chapel – a single wall, 12 feet high, made of chalk and stone.

Cross carefully at the junction with the main road and go straight ahead to enter East Ravendale.

7. From the thatched cottage continue straight on at the fork and, passing The Elms on your left, take the footpath over a field to join a fine avenue of trees bisecting farm buildings. A short distance to your right this avenue is barred by a gate, beyond which the footpath bends left along a good track. When you have passed woods on both your right and left you realise you have arrived at the top of the world! Below you is a vast panorama embracing the whole of the coastal plain and the Humber Estuary as far as Spurn Lighthouse in distant Yorkshire. The track deteriorates to a field path before descending once more to Barton Street, where you turn left.

8. After a few yards another footpath is indicated on your right. This takes you down the hillside on a wide grassy track. This route comes to an end at a tall hedge, but you will spot a gap in the hedges to your right. Through this gap pass a muddy farm track on your left before reaching a kissing-gate. Through this a clear track leads you over a meadow of long grass to yet another kissing-gate and into Post Office Lane in Ashby-cum-Fenby. You are soon on the road in the centre of the village, where, to your left, a short walk takes you past a chapel to the entrance drive into Hall Farm, and the teashop.

Walk 20
CLEETHORPES

Lincolnshire is very much a coastal county, and this walk combines many interesting aspects of life next to the sea. Beginning at the most up-to-date teashop in Cleethorpes, part of the spectacular Discovery Centre building, the route leads you along the coast as far as open countryside, crossing the Greenwich Meridian and passing through an up-market 'shanty town'. Different paths then return you to Boaters, displaying some of the attractions of a popular seaside resort – a large theme park, a narrow-gauge steam railway, and a delightful boating lake shared by rowing boats, fishermen and many types of birds.

☕ Cleethorpes Discovery Centre looks almost surreal in its traditional setting by the Boating Lake, ducks rippling the surface of the water and moored rowing boats bobbing gently up and down. It is a stunning new building, a circle of high white panels rising to a small upper gallery and topped by a tiny spire. The design is ambitious and brave, as is the 'Time' Exhibition housed on the upper deck. Behind the wall of glass at ground level is Boaters Tea Rooms, where you will be treated to an excellent lunch, morning coffee or afternoon tea. From here you can gaze out at the trees and wildlife around the shores and islands of the lake – even better in fine weather, when the glass doors open out onto the 'piazza'. Most of the food is freshly baked here, and what is not is supplied by only the finest bakers. An original choice of tasty main meals features pastas, cheeses and a quiche to die for. 'Boaters Melts' enjoy the same high standing – filled baguettes grilled with a cheese topping. Follow this with toffee apple crumble or home-made fruit pie, and finish by choosing from an array of teas, coffees and hot chocolates. In addition a specials blackboard always features a fresh soup of the day – who could ask for more? Telephone: 01472 200672. Opening hours are straightforward – 10 am to 5 pm every day – but if you miss Boaters, close-by Cleethorpes offers all the options you would expect from a busy seaside resort.

DISTANCE: 4½ miles.
MAPS: OS Landranger 113 (Grimsby) or Explorer 284.
STARTING POINT: The Discovery Centre at the Boating Lake in Cleethorpes (GR 318075).
HOW TO GET THERE: From Cleethorpes town centre follow Kingsway south-east along the coast. Past the Leisure Centre this road becomes the King's Road, and after half a mile you turn left at a mini-roundabout to enter a large car park adjacent to the Discovery Centre.
ALTERNATIVES: You could park at Anthony's Bank to begin the walk from a different place (point 3). Extend the walk by including an expedition into Cleethorpes or to the far extent of the Fitties. Be sure to include a trip on the steam railway if the trains are running!

THE WALK
1. From Boaters walk behind the Discovery Centre to cross a green metal bridge over the Boating Lake. Then carefully over the narrow-gauge railway line to join the coastal path, turning right onto this, with sand dunes and dense gorse on your left. Over the dunes marvellous wide views open up of the whole of the Humber Estuary and the North Sea beyond, of ships of all shapes and sizes going to and from the ports along the Humber, and of the old black and white lighthouse at Spurn Point on the opposite bank. Half a mile along this path you come to a curious metal plate set in the tarmac across the footway – the inscription tells you that you have reached the Greenwich Meridian.

East meets west, so to speak, at the Greenwich Meridian, established in

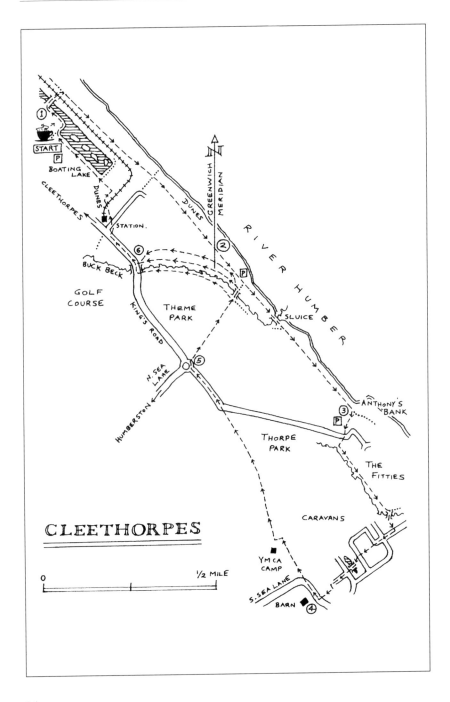

CLEETHORPES

0   ½ MILE

1884 as the standard for time reckoning throughout the world. In the early 1930s the metal plate was presented by a Sheffield foundry and set across the pathway to test a new non-corroding steel. Its condition today pays tribute to the quality of the metal. The nearby signpost tells you that you are 9,919 miles from the South Pole but only 2,517 from the North.

2. Stepping boldly into the East continue along your way, and cross the outfall of Buck Beck. Do not be tempted down from the path at this point. A combination of deep muddy creeks, shifting sand banks and fast-moving tides make the sands below you a dangerous no-go area which can confound even the most confident navigator. Eventually the track runs out at Anthony's Bank, a good vantage point to inspect the two mysterious grey hulks clearly visible in the estuary. These are Haile Sand Fort and the more distant Bull Sand Fort, the last remains of wartime fortifications guarding the mouth of the river.

3. Now walk across the car park to the road, on the opposite side of which a sign indicates a footpath along the top of an embankment and into the heart of an area known as the Fitties.

'Fitties' comes from the Norse 'fitty' meaning meadowland on the banks of the sea. Humberston Fitties sprang up in the first half of the 20th century as an area of summer holiday homes. Today it is a fascinating maze of unique wooden huts and bungalows, all with a distinctly maritime flavour and each one immaculately maintained. Often unfairly described as a shanty town these charming old wooden structures are sadly giving way to more permanent ones.

Where the embankment curves left descend to a white footbridge and follow the path to a metalled road. Turn right onto this and, when the road bends right, you instead go straight ahead across the grass between a sea of old caravans. Cross a road into an area of more modern caravans, then a bridge across a small lake which leads to another short road. At the end of this road cut between the caravans towards the top left hand corner of the field. Here you find yourself expelled onto South Sea Lane at the edge of open countryside, next to an old tumbledown barn made of red corrugated iron.

4. Follow this road right for just a few yards and when the road curves left through trees, you take the clear track straight ahead of you, to pass the old YMCA camp on your left. This sandy path leads on for ½ mile with pine trees shielding row after row of caravans on your right and excellent views to Humberston church and the Lincolnshire Wolds on the other flank. Through a gate you meet a road serving the caravan parks – continue ahead until you reach the roundabout at the entrance to the Pleasure Island theme park.

Pleasure Island has risen from the ashes of the old Cleethorpes Marineland and Zoo. With a lifespan of less than twenty years the zoo closed in 1979 amid an outcry of protest against the rumoured appalling conditions suffered by the last remaining animals there. Reportedly unfed, uncleaned and uncared for, the plight of these forgotten animals was in sharp contrast to that of Hercules the hippo, who became a local celebrity as a new home had been sought for him a few months earlier.

5. Avoid the main road at this point by following a forgotten lane on your right which overlooks many of the attractions of the theme park. At the bridge choose between attractive paths on either side of Buck Beck, or climb the wooded bank to follow a high-level path above the stream, offering you excellent views of the park's most breathtaking features. All three routes lead you to the same point on King's Road near a golf range.

6. Follow King's Road to the miniature Lakeside Station, neatly painted in cream and green to recreate the atmosphere of a bygone era of steam. This is the terminus of the Cleethorpes Coast Light Railway, and, unless you are lured into taking the train back towards the Discovery Centre, your path passes to the right of the station and over the narrow track itself into more sand dunes.

The area of Cleethorpes beach and the sand dunes is a wildlife habitat of national importance and in 1988 the dunes were designated as a Site of Special Scientific Interest, together with saltflats and mudflats further down the coast. As well as a home for numerous rare plants this is a key point for thousands of birds using Cleethorpes as a stop-off point on the 'East Atlantic Flyway'. The teeming life in the mud feeds grey plover, dunlin and knot among others heading as far as South Africa.

The way now continues clearly through the dunes and over grass to the Boating Lake again. From here a simple lakeside walk takes you past the bandstand and a rather sad castellated outhouse to the Discovery Centre once more. If you still have time to spare, there are boats to be hired, ducks and geese to be fed, and 'Caught much?' to be shouted to young anglers trying to tempt bream, tench or pike.